DEDICATION

This book is dedicated to the memory of my father DAVID CRAIG (Evangelist), example and encourager.

4

Contents

6

Preface

This is a story about living people and contemporary events. It is about people who laugh and cry, sing and pray, have their ups and downs, just like us. The only difference is that they happen to live in Romania.

The decade 1984-1994 was unique in Romanian history, encompassing the five years before, and the five years after the Revolution.

This is a very personal account of those ten years; but it also includes, of necessity, some events prior to that period, and a brief update of the testimony for God in Romania after 1994.

I have, to the best of my ability, checked the authenticity of the facts which I have related. Some of my readers will recognise the part which they played, either in prayer, practical help, or their presence with the Christians in Romania. I hope that, with me, they will acknowledge the Sovereignty of God and His faithfulness to His people.

There are many other friends working for the Lord in Romania who are not mentioned, and I trust they will not think unkindly of me. I have spoken only of those things with which I was intimately connected.

The Christian testimony in Romania is undergoing a very intensive and rapid change. It is difficult to envisage what will transpire in the next decade, if our Lord has not come. However, I am satisfied that some kind of line can be drawn at 1994 without prejudicing current or future events.

In writing this account, it is my prayer that God's people will have a better insight into lesser known aspects of Romanian life; and how one individual was affected, to his eternal good.

Dundonald
August 1995

Foreword

For more than thirty years, as I have travelled across the frontiers of Eastern Europe, I have realised how relevant is this statement: *"Man builds barriers because he is afraid; God builds bridges because He loves us"*. In this amazing story, you will discover that a bridge of love and hope has been made by the Lord from Northern Ireland, reaching into the hearts and lives of so many people in Romania.

It was not a coincidence, but by providence, that I met Drew and his wife Georgie at Herne Bay Court in Kent during the summer of 1980. They were on holiday, and I was responsible for the ministry of God's Word. Later I received an invitation to visit Northern Ireland, where I shared about the trials and triumphs of the suffering church in the Communist countries.

And so it was that, in May 1984, Drew and I journeyed to Eastern Europe, trusting the Lord in every situation. We experienced wonderful fellowship together and with the believers, the reality of prayer, and the impact of the gospel. Sometimes we were in danger, and afraid; especially waiting at the borders, uncertain of what was going to happen; or when we were under constant surveillance by the Secret Police. Truly there was protection from the Lord.

Now I should like to mention Doina from Sibiu, who is a gifted translator in the services and in the homes. I can recall one occasion when we were in Blaj. The church was filled to capacity, the congregation sang the hymns with enthusiasm, and prayed fervently. There were three speakers: Drew from Northern Ireland, a brother from Scotland, and myself from England - all with different accents and styles of preaching. Assisted by the Holy Spirit, Doina translated the messages with such an anointing for nearly two hours.

I also recall the time we visited the synagogue in Sibiu, and engaged in lively conversation with the elderly leader. Whilst he was showing us the beautiful Torah scrolls, I asked him quietly, "Do you believe in the coming of the Messiah?". Suddenly his manner became threatening, and we were alarmed! When he had calmed down, he agreed to accept a copy of a bi-lingual New Testament in Hebrew/Romanian.

Then there was the visit to the home of brother Moldoveanu, a famous composer of the words and music of more than one thousand Romanian hymns. For his loyalty to Christ, he was imprisoned for six years, and also tortured. In these terrible conditions the Lord gave him "songs in the night". The Bible and writing materials were forbidden; but with the aid of a broken piece of glass and pieces of soap he wrote three hundred hymns, which he taught to some of his fellow-prisoners. On his release, Christians from all over the country would come to his house and stay a few days, patiently copying by hand these melodies of inspiration.

What are the main characteristics of the Christians in Romania, who have learned that they are not meant to be the victims of circumstances, but rather victors through the love of God?

* Conviction in the authority of the Scriptures.
* Experience of the power of prayer.
* Belief that the Lord Jesus Christ is supreme and sufficient.
* A living hope in the coming of Christ.

Reading this fascinating testimony, you will be aware of the presence and power of the Lord in His church today. The events recorded will be a challenge. Will you consider your response?

May the Lord motivate you into prayer, support and action.

Gerald Gotzen
Torquay
June 1995

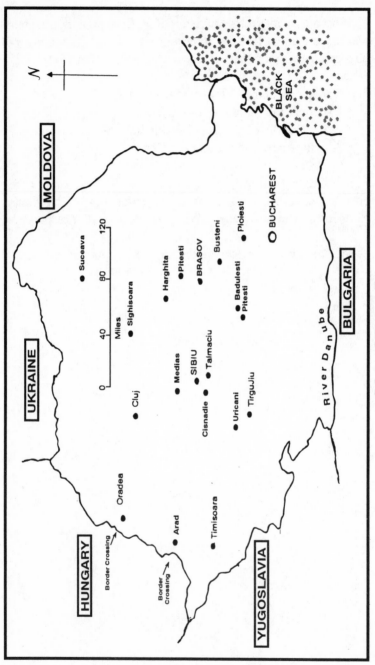

Map of Romania

Introduction

NOT ACROSS THE SEAS

From early childhood I attended missionary meetings, and became familiar with the maps of India, Argentina, Brazil, Belgian Congo, and many others. The repeated call to see *"fields ... white already to harvest"* (John 4:35), and the scarcity of labourers, caused me great anxiety and inner conflict.

It was only in later years I realised that the Lord's discussion with His disciples was in the context of the fields in Samaria - which were not across the seas, but just down the road!

While the disciples went for food, the Master rested on a well. On that well, He 'ploughed a field', 'sowed a seed', and 'reaped a harvest'! *"Come,"* she cried, *"see a man, who told me all things that ever I did: is not this the Christ?"* The first recorded missionary to Samaria was a woman. The extent of her travel with the good news was within walking distance of where she first heard it.

As a teenager in the Autumn of 1947 I listened to three young men tell of the Lord's call in their lives, and of their imminent departure for India. I was deeply moved in that meeting, and felt that, perhaps, one day I too would cross the seas to a distant land in the Lord's service. Until that night, and for many more years, I believed that the definition of a "Missionary" was one who went to a foreign country with the gospel to see people brought to the Saviour, and indigenous churches established; and "Evangelists" were those who did the same kind of work in their own countries.

It never occurred to me that the Lord was preparing a mission field for me thirty miles from where I had been brought up. I did not go to India; it was in Dundonald, County Down, that I was to serve the Lord for over forty years.

However, those youthful ambitions were known to the Lord and, in 1984, He gave entrance to another field that was to take me much further from home.

In the 'Samaritan fields' message, the Master had said to His disciples, *"I sent you to reap that whereon you bestowed no labour: other men laboured, and you are entered into their labours"*. This new field was one for which I had not laboured; I had not prayed for it, nor given anything to it. I knew it was in Eastern Europe, and that its capital was Bucharest. That was all!

CHAPTER I

"Great Doors Swing On Small Hinges"

I t was Henry Law, the Bible expositor, who used this expression. When Joseph asked the butler in the Egyptian prison-house *"Why do you look so sad today?"* that was the hinge that eventually opened the door for Joseph. It took him from the prison to the palace, and altered the whole course of his life.

For myself, it was a question asked in a car park in Kent, England, in September 1980, that opened a door of opportunity for me to travel in Eastern Europe. "Have you ever been to Northern Ireland?", I asked. The question was impulsive, instant.

Gerald Gotzen had been the guest speaker at Herne Bay Court Christian Conference Centre and Holiday Home for that week. My wife, Georgie, and I had listened each morning and evening to the Lord's servant. We were deeply impressed. His talks in the morning on the Word of God re-sharpened my tired mind, and rekindled a flagging spirit. In the evenings we 'travelled' from East Germany to Siberia, and also took in Israel and Ethiopia! Gerald did not appeal for workers; but pleaded for prayer for the work, which was difficult, dangerous, highly rewarding, and so much in need. This was the burden of a really selfless servant of God.

It was not only what he said that spoke to me; but how he said it. I had the growing, deepening conviction that this man was one of the Lord's special messengers. I had received a blessing, and I wanted the folk in my own church to receive it as well. Hence, the question, "Have you ever been to Northern Ireland?". As with Joseph, it was to make a change in me, affect my home, my friends, and many people in Ireland and further afield. It would bring me into a new, precious relationship and fellowship with Eastern European Christians. But all this was still in the Lord's safe-keeping.

It took a few seconds for the question to register. Then, with a smile and very gently, the answer came: "No, I've never been to Northern Ireland!".

"Would you be able to come some time, and share with us some of the things we have been listening to this week?", I continued.

He paused, then said, "I'll pray about it. Perhaps you would give me your address and, if the Lord opens the way, I will be in touch." We shook hands, and parted.

Georgie and I got into our car and drove to High Wycombe to meet Philip and Heather Saunders, from our fellowship in Dundonald, who were at the Wycliffe Bible Translation Centre preparing to serve the Lord among the Kouya people of the Ivory Coast. We shared with them what we had enjoyed at Herne Bay Court, and agreed that it would be good if Gerald could find time to come to Brooklands. "It might", Heather suggested, "inspire some of the young folk to serve the Lord, there or elsewhere." It came as a bit of a bombshell, when they later found out that I was the one the Lord had spoken to!

Early in 1981 I received a letter from Gerald. He had ten days free, and would be happy to take up the invitation to come to Northern Ireland. Two visits followed, in 1981 and 1983. The in-depth reports of the Eastern European Christians' desperate struggle for survival, their urgent need for the basic necessities for life, and the remarkable progress of the Evangelical churches - particularly in Romania - made a deep impression on everyone.

Before Gerald left our home in 1983, he had a question: "Would you like to come with me on one of my visits to Eastern Europe? I could introduce you to leaders in the Brethren churches, and I am sure they would be greatly encouraged by your presence and help in the Word of God. They have very little fellowship with other Christians, and just to know that believers from the West are interested in them, would be a real blessing."

"Think about it, and we will pray that it may be possible. We could either fly to Bucharest and hire a little Dacia car, or you could join me in England and we could travel in my car through the various countries, staying with people I know. I think we would need at least two weeks for this, and perhaps a little longer!"

The door had opened just a little wider!

During the remainder of 1983 my mind often returned to the proposed trip. I was heavily committed in our own fellowship; and there never seemed to be a 'right time' to take on additional responsibilities. There were a-hundred-and-one valid reasons why I should not get involved. So I prayed for peace in my heart - whichever way the Lord would lead. I realised I could find no Scripture that would prevent me from going. It was down to circumstances and inner contentment: the well-preached and proven formula for guidance.

The matter came to a head in February 1984, when I received a firm proposition from Gerald, with dates in May. Now I was under intense pressure. Georgie said to me, "You should think carefully about what you're taking on". It was practical and necessary advice!

I said, "Well, it's just one visit. I need only get involved as much as I am able; but it would be a shame to miss this unique opportunity." I continued, "Gerald received substantial financial help for Eastern Europe from the Christians when he was here, and there are people praying now for the situation, who knew nothing about it before. If they heard about this proposed visit, I am sure they would be more than willing to contribute towards the great need".

I talked and prayed with my fellow elders, and dispatched a note to Gerald. I told him that I was willing to take up his offer, and would like to go overland. In this way I could meet a cross section of people, and bring them some practical, as well as spiritual, sustenance. I then contacted ten Christian businessmen, who I knew would have a personal interest in this venture; they were also elders in their respective churches.

Within six weeks - just one week before I was due to leave - a total of six thousand pounds dropped through my letter box! It was confirmation, but also frightening! And only the firstfruits of a great harvest that was to follow.

CHAPTER II

Crossing The Frontier

"Brother," said Gerald, "I don't know how I am going to get these cases into my car. It's already full!" This was the down-to-earth greeting that awaited me at Gatwick Airport.

"Well," I replied, "I had a lot of talking to do at Belfast to get it all on board without having to pay excess baggage. I told them that I was on a special assignment to Eastern Europe, and it was very important that I got all the baggage through with as little extra expense as possible!" So we spent the next half-hour unloading, re-loading, adjusting, pushing and pulling, until everything was safely in the car. The only problem was, there was very little room left for my rather long legs! The back of the car was dangerously close to the road, and the front was looking heavenward!

"We'll have to drive with great care", Gerald said; and I could see he was a little uneasy as we turned south for Dover. But we were on our way!

We arrived in Southern Germany on the Saturday evening, and visited the local Brethren church in Schwabach on Sunday morning. Our host was a Romanian who had recently been repatriated to West Germany. His brother, still in Romania, was to be our main contact.

"What majestic scenery!" I remarked, as we drove through Austria. The snow-capped, lordly Alps, the high, wispy clouds in a dark blue sky; but I was not in a holiday mood. Something of the importance of this journey stirred within me, and I was not totally relaxed. We by-passed Vienna - or Wien as I was to know it - and in what seemed a very short time we approached the Hungarian border. Gerald had made this journey often before, but I was about to breach the Iron Curtain for the first time!

Three parallel lines of high wire, separated by one hundred metres of mined no-man's-land dominated by high wooden observation towers, marked the frontier. A sullen soldier asked for our passports and inspected them. Looking at us in turn, he motioned us to proceed to the next check point, where the performance was repeated; then we were directed to line up at the Customs Post proper. We did not have transit visas for Hungary, so we waited in line with our photographs. There were no hitches, and two hours later we drove through the final barrier. We were in Eastern Europe.

The 'mission' had begun!

Our plan was to spend as long as possible in Romania, and allow time to have a weekend in Czechoslovakia on our return journey; so we were able to spend just one night in Budapest, in the home of a very gentle and dear couple. He was the pastor of a small church, and his wife was a medical doctor. He took us to the Police Station where we registered for the overnight stay, and obtained permission to sleep in his home. After a really needed meal we read the Scriptures, had a short discussion and prayed. We were shown to our sleeping quarters, which I guessed was their only bedroom. Our host bade us Goodnight and, just before he closed the door, he turned and said with a smile "you will not be troubled tonight by the police, so sleep well!". He was right, and we did!

The next morning the sun shone with a pure brilliance. I looked at my watch: it was six o'clock and I was wide awake, so I spent the next hour reading and writing. Then it was time for breakfast. My first night in a Communist land was over. We stood together with our host and his wife and commended them and ourselves to the Lord. We said Good-bye, turned east and headed for the Romanian border.

Four hours later we were there. At last! It had taken us four days. Gerald pulled the car into the side of the road. There was something different about him - his demeanour had changed.

"You know, Drew," he said, "I have been travelling into Romania for nearly twenty years, and I never know what to expect. Sometimes I have had to wait for hours, in much prayer because of the hostile atmosphere; I have been searched, interrogated, and have had some of the goods confiscated. I've even been turned back!"

That was all I needed to hear, and my heart began to thump! To have come all this distance, after all the prayer and preparation, only to be turned back or to have the goods confiscated - it didn't bear thinking about. "Let's hope that, at the worst, we just have to pay duty", I volunteered bravely!

We were now about half a mile from the frontier. It was 11.45 G.M.T. on the 12th May 1984. Gerald checked through his papers, having a last look for any offending item. When he was satisfied that all was in order, he turned to me and said, "Let us read Psalm 121 - the traveller's Psalm, then we will ask for the Lord's protection".

So I began *"I will lift up my eyes to the hills ..."*.

After I had read the first two verses he said to me, "Do you know, this is really a question?".

"No", I replied.

So he continued, *"Will I lift up my eyes to the hills? Does my help come from there? No! My help comes from the Lord, the Creator of the heavens and the earth ..."*.

I finished reading the Psalm, *"... the Lord shall preserve thy going out and thy coming in from this time forth, and even for evermore"*. AMEN! PRAISE THE LORD!

Then we closed our eyes. I tried to pray, but couldn't find any words. Suddenly I remembered that a few Christian friends from my home church would be praying about these frontier crossings. I felt reassured and, out loud, thanked the Lord for them, and for bringing us this far. Together, we placed ourselves into His hands. He was Sovereign, not the Communist authorities further up the road.

We must trust Him, and not be afraid.

After Gerald had commended us to the Lord he started the engine and we drove to the double barrier at the frontier. Both the Hungarian and Romanian border guards inspected our passports. We were then directed to proceed to the Customs station - a foreboding, soul-less place. We followed the signs for Western vehicles. Our car was the only one in this lane. Beside us were many Eastern European vehicles: old bangers of all shapes and sizes. They were being systematically searched; and it was obvious, from the tears of the women and the gesticulations and loud protestations of the men, that all was not well for some of them.

I began a mental audit of what we had in our car: boxes of food and clothing, two drive shafts for Skoda cars, engine oil, our luggage, including my six cases, personal recorders, cameras, films, etc.! I just didn't know what was going to happen! We sat for one hour, and nobody came to us. We kept ourselves occupied by listening to Alan Parks, the North American singer's tape, "Hymns I grew up with". We sang, or tried to sing, "My Redeemer! Oh what beauties in that lovely name appear ...", and other well-known worship hymns.

Then they came: two uniformed Customs officers, one Hungarian and one Romanian. I recall noticing how immaculate the Hungarian looked in comparison with his dowdy Romanian counterpart. Stepping up to the car, the Romanian barked "Passports, please!".

CHAPTER III

The Forgotten School Bag

A few days before I left home to travel to Romania, a Christian lady in Belfast asked me, "Could you possibly take a little parcel for me to my friend Lidia in Bucharest?". Was this another key-question? It proved to be so. "Certainly!" I replied, "It will be a pleasure. Make sure you give me her address and telephone number."

The 'parcel' duly arrived at my home. It was one of those brightly coloured school satchels, not the sort of thing I had expected to carry. Lidia had two young children, a girl and a boy. The school bag was for the boy and the contents were for the others. I took a note of their address and telephone number. "We will do our best to deliver these", I assured my friend. She replied that, if it became too difficult to make contact with Lidia, we could give it to someone else.

In the final packing I put the school bag in my brief case, along with other small personal items, and forgot about it. But now I was to be reminded about it in an unexpected way.

After we had handed over our passports we waited for what seemed an age. I could feel the pressure build up inside me as we continued to play our hymns, and I prayed silently that the Lord would give me faith to believe that everything would be all right. Eventually the same Customs official returned and, without introductions or any small talk, he ordered us to empty the vehicle. "You want us to take EVERYTHING out?" Gerald enquired gently.

"Yes, EVERYTHING!" he said, emphasising "everything".

"It's raining!" I said to Gerald, "the food in the boxes will get wet." But there was no response from him; he had already opened the boot and was setting the contents on to the pavement. I joined in and, as we unloaded under the watchful eyes of the Romanian and Hungarian officials, I could feel the resentment building up inside me. I am thankful that the "Traveller's Psalm" was in my heart, and the Lord quietened my spirit. We emptied the car, both inside and outside, using blankets we had with us to protect the most vulnerable goods from the rain.

Earlier I had noticed four large signs suspended above our heads. They conveyed the same message in four languages, the English saying "Welcome to hospitable Romania"! I had passed some caustic comment to Gerald about how ironic it was, but now we would just have to take things as they came.

I certainly had not reckoned on what was to follow. As it happened, I lifted out my brief case last, and handed it to the Romanian. He opened it, and there was the school bag - the only bright thing about the place! I had completely forgotten about it.
"Is this yours?" he said, pointing.
"No, not really", I replied.
"Then who does it belong to?"
"A friend gave it to me. It's a present for a family", I ventured.
"What's in it?"

"I don't know", I responded, as my pulse rate increased!

"Well, I want to know", he continued, in a slightly agitated tone, as he reached for the buckles.

He opened it and unceremoniously turned it upside-down. A variety of items fell out on to the wet road. Some of them didn't worry me, they comprised small items of clothing. But, to my horror, on the ground, I recognised a scattered bundle of Dr. de Haan's Bible Study notes and a paperback book. I immediately stooped to pick them up. "Leave them!", the Customs officer said sternly. He proceeded to lift them, one at a time. Unhurriedly, he flipped through every page and put them in a pile on the roof of the very wet car! He lifted the book last, and I could see Gerald strain to read the cover. I realised he was shocked and annoyed; and he had every right to be, because he had specifically told me not to bring any literature.

"Just an unmarked Bible for your own use", had been his instruction.

On top of the uncertainty of what would happen next, I now felt really miserable. I had failed Gerald; failed him, at the very beginning of our trip. I felt ashamed, guilty. I was an inexperienced intruder into this work of the Lord's servant. Would this put him in jeopardy? Would it affect his future missions? This was his work for the Lord. For me, it was the first, and maybe the last, visit. These and many more questions passed through my mind in a few seconds.

The Customs Officer said, "I'm sorry, you cannot take these with you. I will give you a receipt, and you can collect them when you return from your visit."

"We are not coming back this way", Gerald interjected.

Before the Customs man had time to reply, I almost shouted, "You can keep them!".

"And read them!", Gerald quipped.

The Hungarian Officer, who had watched passively until then, broke into a sarcastic laugh, and said "Him! He wouldn't read them. He's an atheist!".

Picking up the book, Gerald quickly retorted, "This book is good for atheists! I know its author, I met her some years ago. It is a remarkable story of the saving and healing power of God in a young woman's life, all because of her belief in the power of the blood of Jesus Christ." He continued to speak the gospel in a forthright and sincere way. It didn't really last long, but it seemed a long time! There was silence. I stood and sweated.

After a long pause, with a faint smile, the Customs Officer said "Sorry, you cannot take them with you. Follow me!"

In single file, we walked the fifty metres or so up to the office: the Official in front, me next, and Gerald somewhere behind. I didn't look round, I didn't have the courage. I had let him down, and I knew he was upset. "Lord," I prayed, "make this work out all right." The Customs hall was dark and musty, not at all an inviting place. A few disconsolate-looking travellers lounged around - no doubt hoping, as we were, that they would soon be on their journey again. There was a number of glass windows, with faded green curtains. The curtains were closed. Our leader pointed to one window, and ordered in a rather onerous voice "Wait there!". We both stood in silence, two unhappy people.

After ten or fifteen minutes - which seemed like an eternity - our Customs man pulled back the curtain and opened the window. He pushed out a receipt-type book with duplicate pages. What was printed on the page was in Romanian, but he indicated a line near the bottom and said "Sign, please". As I bent down to do this I looked through the window, into the office. It was a spacious room with desks ranged in rows. At each desk there was a uniformed official. Each one of them had a Bible Study booklet! They were totally engrossed in what they were reading. In a flash I turned to Gerald and said "Look in there!". I signed the paper, the Official tore it out and handed it to me without speaking. He closed the window, and pulled the curtain over.

As we turned to walk to the car, Gerald broke the uneasy silence. "The Lord has overruled. If I had known that you had those books with you, we would have left them in Hungary. But these people will read and re-read them. They are hungry for Western literature, of any sort; and they will likely pass them on to others. We must pray that the Lord will use them to bring these people to faith in Christ." I do not know whether that prayer has been answered; at least, not yet.

Quite suddenly, Spring had arrived in my heart! I was so relieved, and I expressed this relief audibly. Gerald simply smiled and said, "We haven't got our passports back yet!". I had forgotten all about my passport, so now my relief was tempered with a little unease. However, I was confident that the Lord would continue to overrule, as he had thus far.

There was no one at the car. The rain had stopped. Earlier I had gathered up the contents of the school bag, put them in, strapped it up and returned it to my briefcase, without the books - they were now on unexpected missions!

No other Western car had joined our lane. We sat on a concrete slab, waiting for the Customs officer and the return of our passports. After some time we decided to get into the car and play more music. The tension was beginning to reappear. Why the delay? Could there be a problem? How much longer would we have to wait? Then we saw him coming down the steps and across the road into the Passport Checking office. But nothing happened. Still the minutes ticked by.

About half-an-hour later he emerged with the open passports in his hand. He came to my side first. The window of the car was already rolled down. Coming close, he straightened himself up and, in a very officious way, began to leaf through my passport. I remember thinking that he must know what's in there off by heart. He stopped at the page with the photograph, looked at me, then looked at it, and said, "Mr. Graag? Your passport! Have a good journey in our country!". Over the years I have discovered that, for some reason, it is difficult for the Europeans to pronounce "Craig". On that first occasion I wasn't too worried - it was such a lovely feeling to have that little black and gold book back in my possession!

He then walked round the front of the car to Gerald's open window where he went through the same procedure, but with a tantalising slowness. Turning and re-turning the pages, he studied some of the Visa stamps. Gerald's passport was like a Who's Who of continental travel! This Official was in no hurry, he was going nowhere and he appeared to be relishing his work! "Have a good journey", he repeated, as he handed the passport over. He stood back, saluted us, turned to the soldier who was manning the barrier ahead and waved to him. We were on our way!

We drove into the May sunshine, passing rows of parked vehicles heading in the opposite direction. After travelling a short distance we pulled into a sort of lay-by, both of us quite exhausted. Rejoicing, we thanked God for our safe entry. The Lord had answered my Nehemiah, instant-type, prayer *"to the God of heaven"* (Neh. 2:4). He had, indeed, worked it out for us.

CHAPTER IV

First Impressions

From the moment we crossed the frontier we moved back in time by eighty to one hundred years. Forlorn groups worked on the land with primitive implements, using oxen, horses in varying conditions of fitness and size, and the majestic buffalo - all in the yoke. They pulled ramshackles that were knocked together as wagons. In the majority of cases these were used for transporting the families of these gypsy-like people, all dressed in drab clothing. Gerald told me that they were not gypsies, just ordinary people in a different world from the one I belonged to.

Storks surveyed the dreary landscape from their massive mushroom-shaped nests perched precariously on the tops of telegraph poles. We negotiated the pot-holed roads - now on the right side, then on the left - weaving our way into Oradea, one of Romania's largest cities, the capital of Bihor region. Only then did it occur to me that, in our relatively short journey from the border, we had seen little vehicular traffic. As there were few direction signs in the city, it was a relief to be with a driver who knew where he was going. He had travelled this road many times before. "You can't ask for directions. It's too dangerous. The Militia, the uniformed and overt arm of the security system, are to be treated with respect, and the less we have to do with them the better", he explained.

Apparently they were not of the friendly British Bobby type!

People moved about the city streets like fugitives, even though they were in their own country. Shops were usually identified by long queues of people. "They'll be waiting for bread or milk, or whatever they can get", Gerald said. "In Russia" he continued, "shoppers carry a little bag with them everywhere they go, and join any queue they see. Do you know what the bag is called?" he asked. "In English it means 'maybe you will, and maybe you won't!'."

There was nothing inviting about these street scenes: no bright clothes, no groups of people chatting; nothing at all that would give the impression of well-being, camaraderie or neighbourliness. As far as the eye could see there were grimy blocks of high-rise apartment buildings. They stood in serried ranks, their balconies bedecked with the family laundry.

Entering Oradea, I had commented on the large bill-board-type signs by the roadside and, in some places, over the road. These were in praise of President Nicolae Ceaucescu. They were accompanied by a plethora of advertisements lauding the Socialist Republic of Romania. In the city itself, and in all the subsequent towns and villages, these messages dominated the vantage points. They were on factory roofs, schools and public buildings. The President's photograph was prominent in every conceivable place. Nobody was allowed to forget whose they were, and whom they served. This was Ceaucescu's Romania!

Gerald told me that there were many Christians in Oradea. "This is where Joseph Tson ministered in a large Baptist church, with a congregation of two thousand five hundred", he said. It was mainly through the courageous efforts of this man in the early

1970's that some degree of liberty was won for the Evangelical communities throughout Romania. He managed to get the government to formally recognise the churches. To obtain this, the churches had to be bound by a strict code of conduct. The situation was difficult and unsatisfactory; but it was better than it had been previously.

Tson was a marked man, harassed and hounded by the Securitate. The government did everything in its power, short of imprisoning him, to stop his ministry. At one stage the pressure was so great that his wife had a nervous breakdown, and the elders of the church pleaded with him to leave the country. "Joseph, they will kill you. Go and work for Romania from America", they pleaded. To this he replied, "And supposing I go to America and get on well in my help for my country; and one day the Lord says to me, 'Joseph, what are you doing here?', I would be miserable. But if I stay here, where I am needed at the present time, even if I am arrested and separated from my beloved wife Elizabeth and put in a prison cell, when I look up into heaven and see my Father smiling, and saying 'Well done, Joseph', I will be happy!".

Soon Oradea was behind us. The road, railway and river meandered together with an enchanting beauty through the beautiful Transylvanian countryside. I was fascinated to stand beside a poorly marked level crossing, and feel the ground shake as a forty-carriage freight train thundered by. This form of transportation was Romania's life-blood. Hairy-cloaked shepherds, who looked as though they hadn't been in bed or washed for many weeks, roamed the open hillsides with their sheep - thousands of them.

After five hours of uninterrupted driving, we arrived in Sibiu, the central city of Transylvania and Romania. Transylvania, reputed home of haunted castles, has had a tumultuous past. For one thousand years, until the First World War, this province was part of Hungary. However, as far back as the thirteenth century its seven principal towns were founded by Saxon merchant men who gave them German names. If you speak to a German-Romanian he will call Sibiu, Hermannstadt, and Transylvania, Siebenburgen!

Sibiu is a beautiful old walled city. With its captivating German style architecture, it is the gateway to the snow-topped Faragas mountains - a section of the Carpathian range - dominated by the highest peak, Mount Moldoveanu, 2544 metres above sea level.

David Stanley, in his tour guide "Eastern Europe on a Shoe-string" says: "If you only visit one Romanian city, make it Sibiu". Happily it was this city that was to be my home-from-home in succeeding visits over the next ten years.

We drove to the Continental Hotel in the centre of the city. It was a modern-looking tower block ten storeys high. My general curiosity of seeing around me was suddenly interrupted by Gerald's comment, as he parked the car: "When we go inside, we must not talk to each other. It's more than likely that there are people listening. Western visitors are a rare commodity in hotels, and they are watched very closely. There may even be listening devices planted, so we must be very careful", he explained. "We will try to book into separate rooms, to reduce any suspicion", he said. At that time, hotel accommodation was very cheap by Western standards, so we felt we were not overdoing it.

The sheep and the shepherds, the tranquil, scenic beauty of the countryside, and all that we had seen since crossing the border five hours before, were now forgotten. We pushed open the revolving door and entered a dimly lit, smoke-filled foyer, bustling with loud-speaking Russians who were about to leave. We could see from the folders they carried that they had been at some kind of seminar or conference. We edged forward to the desk as unobtrusively as we could and set down our cases. With a disarming smile, Gerald asked in English, "Can we have two rooms, please?".

CHAPTER V

Room 109

T he question was addressed to a masculine-looking, uniformed lady. Without a comment or a smile, she pushed
two registration forms towards us. They were full sheet
size. I followed Gerald line by line, like a schoolboy, as he filled
in the required details. We never spoke. When completed, we
handed the forms back to the receptionist.

We had received a special authorisation paper at the frontier,
permitting us to stay seven nights in Romania. The document
certified that we had exchanged dollars for the local currency, the
lei: so much for each night's stay. Out of this and every other such
transaction, the Romanian authorities made a hefty profit.

Our inflexible receptionist scrutinised the forms; then we
changed more money and bought petrol coupons. This was one of
the few ways to obtain fuel. The fuel stations in each city were
tightly controlled, and no money was legally tendered there.
Coupons had to be purchased at the frontier, at a police station, or
in a hotel. There was no limit to what we could buy, as these were
bought with foreign currency, which was of great value to this

bankrupt country. We bought many more than we needed for our immediate use. It was our intention to pass them on to the few people in the churches who had vehicles, and who used them mainly in the Lord's work.

At that time the ration per month, for those who could afford it, was the equivalent of six gallons. This could be obtained only at the station where they were registered. As the authorities did not seem to mind their own people having 'tourist coupons', these were of great value to the Christians, who shared them with others. Any fuel station in any part of the country would accept them, so they could now travel to the more remote parts of their country, to visit and have fellowship with other churches. This was a real bonus!

When all the transactions were successfully accomplished at the desk, we were handed our keys. Gerald's room number was 99, and mine 109. We negotiated our way to the lift, pressed the bell, opened the door and piled in our baggage. The lift was small and very dark. We ascended in silence. Gerald got out at the ninth floor, and I went on up to the tenth.

Before leaving the car we had agreed to have a wash, transfer some gifts from our luggage into plastic bags, and meet each other in the foyer in half an hour. As I walked along the dreary corridor I passed at least two bedrooms. Their doors were opened wide to the wall, and they appeared to be unoccupied.

Room 109 will be imprinted on my mind as long as I live! The musty smell, the peeling wallpaper, heavy drab curtains, bulky old fashioned furniture, and, very much out of its era, a large TV set. The room was en suite! No plugs in the bath or wash-hand-basin, tiles broken, chipped or missing, no light in the bathroom, and one tiny bar of rough soap. My attention was taken up with the toilet paper! It was a dark brown colour, and you could see traces of wood shavings engrained in it. Even with gentle handling it tore into holes! Seven nights here? I thought seven minutes would be more than enough!

Half an hour later I closed and locked the door, walked to the stairs past the same two empty rooms, down a flight of stairs, and retraced the same path at a lower level to Gerald's room. Again, I noticed that there were empty rooms. It wasn't until later in the night that I realised my bedroom was directly above his. Why, I wondered, were we not in adjacent rooms on the same floor? We proceeded to the foyer, weaved our way to the desk through the still-chattering Russians, handed in our keys to the same receptionist, and left.

I was on my way to meet my first Romanian Christian friends.

CHAPTER VI

Angels From Heaven

"You wait in the car while I check that everything is all right for us to visit", Gerald said, as we parked in the unlit street. There had been no twilight, and the absence of street lights made for an eerie darkness. Everything was so still. Now and again a shadowy figure would suddenly appear, and then just as quickly disappear. It was to be one of the many times that I could almost hear my heartbeat!

After twenty long minutes Gerald returned. "Yes, it's all right, Drew. We can park the car at the back of Fritz's house. He doesn't want a Western car to be seen at the front. He is under increasing surveillance by the secret police", he explained. "Sorry I was so long, but we got caught up in conversation!" Without lights, we drove to the back of the house, and took out our plastic bags. Immediately, in the darkness, I was embraced with a bear-like hug. He spoke no words, but I could just see the glint of a tear. He was weeping.

Entering the little house, we went through to a room that was a sitting, dining and bedroom. There was really very little walking space, but we sat down - one on each side of the table. In Romania the place for conversation and fellowship is at the table.

Fritz, my new Christian friend, was a German-Romanian, and he conversed with Gerald in German. He was tall and dark, with a sallow complexion. His conversation was punctuated by pauses. He was visibly nervous, and very tense. He gave us an update on the situation in the city, and in the Assembly of Christians where he was one of the leading elders.

I cannot understand German, but I could see that the discussion was taking a lot out of him. After some time, Gerald gave me a summary of the conversation. Fritz had been telling him about their problems and how very difficult things were, but that the Lord was working and many were coming to Christ. Gerald explained to him that he had brought me to have fellowship, bring the greetings of the Brethren churches in Northern Ireland, and also to provide some financial assistance where it was most needed.

"But you must preach!", Fritz exclaimed with a smile. "We want you to share the Word of God with us!" His face was now a picture of radiance, as he reached across the table and squeezed the back of my hand. This was a bonding in brotherly love that has remained unbroken: we have been close friends ever since.

After a little while the door bell rang. Fritz was startled. He looked at his watch and, lifting his eyebrows and hands at the same time, said quietly "Excuse me", and left the room. He was away for nearly half an hour. Gerald and I sat there looking at each other in total silence. In our own way, we both were silently asking the Lord for help and (I know, for myself) calmness. The door eventually opened and Fritz returned with a burly, curly-haired young man, whom he introduced as Morariu (the family name), "the Youth Leader". They both sat down. Now all four sides of the table were occupied. Our new friend sat with lowered head and nervously rubbed his hands together.

"We have a problem", Fritz said. "We hired a bus for tomorrow afternoon, to take our young people to sing and speak at a new church up the country. It is not a 'registered' church. They have only a small number, and we wish to encourage them. We arranged the bus unofficially through a mutual friend and paid the money, which had been gathered up over the previous six months. Today the security police found out about it, and ordered the manager to double the cost. So it is now not possible for us to go. The brother here is very disappointed, and we know it will be an unhappy surprise for our young people."

After all this had been translated for me, I asked how much the additional amount was. They did some calculations, and it worked out at about fifteen U.S. dollars. We were able to give the money needed and, amid tears and embraces, all four of us got down on our knees to thank the Lord for the resolution of the problem. With a broad smile, Fritz said "We call Christians from the West 'angels from heaven'. You never know when they will arrive, and they always bring good news!"

In that room, in completely alien surroundings, I began a journey of intimacy with the Lord, and with the Romanian Christians, such as I had never before experienced. We had some coffee and cake, provided by Fritz's wife, Letitia - a very special little lady with a captivating smile. When we had finished we stood up and briefly commended the situation to the Lord, asking for his special protection during the time we would be together. We left for our hotel at around 10.30 p.m. I was excited and on edge. I couldn't wait until the next morning, when I would meet with the Christians at the Breaking of Bread. We were to be there for nine o'clock.

We parked our very conspicuous car at the hotel's front door and entered the foyer, which was still dimly lit but empty. Behind the desk was a rather rough-looking, heavily moustached man. He lifted the keys from their hooks and when we reached him he handed Gerald the keys to Room 99, and me the keys to 109. In good English, he curtly greeted us, "Goodnight, gentlemen".

Silently, we went up in the lift, and said our 'Goodnights' on the ninth floor. Having completed my journey to the tenth floor, I groped my way along the unlit corridor to Room 109. I fumbled with the key in the lock, opened the door, switched on the light, closed the curtains and had a look around the room. It felt decidedly chilly, so I quickly undressed and was in bed in a few minutes.

I heard my heart again! From underneath the blankets I spoke out to the Lord. I felt alone and homesick, all in one confused, emotional outburst. Then I got to thinking about the keys. How did he know to whom to give the correct keys, without asking? He had not been at the desk when we returned them earlier.

It had been a long first day in Romania, so much had transpired. The episode at the frontier seemed like days ago. I thought a lot about home, Georgie, all the comforts and privileges we enjoyed. I asked the Lord to deepen the work of his Spirit in my life, and confessed my sin of casual living. I turned over and over in my mind what the Lord had said about *"the narrow way that leads to life"*.

Eventually weariness overcame me and I fell asleep!

CHAPTER VII

"Jesus In The Midst"

N ext morning we were the only two in the shabby dining room. I asked Gerald if they had a menu. "I shouldn't think so", he replied with a wry smile. When the waiter came, he asked him what we could have. "We can have eggs, cheese and yoghurt; but there's no tea or coffee!" I chose the eggs and cheese. I was able to eat the eggs, or rather the egg, but I left the cheese. It was sheep's cheese, and just too strong for my palate to endure! There was also some Romanian bread, which I found quite acceptable, although it was a little firm.

Breakfast over, we gathered up our plastic bags, which were to prove indispensable items, and left. On our way to the morning service we discussed the events of the previous evening: the keys, the bedrooms being just above each other. Our immediate thought was that we were being watched.

On a subsequent visit this was verified to us, when we talked to a Christian electronics engineer who had actually been employed to install listening devices in special rooms reserved for foreign travellers.

We arrived at the church just before 9.00 a.m. There was no one about, and only two other cars outside the building. Such a contrast to home, where the car parks overflow with all makes, sizes and shapes of vehicles!

I thought to myself that there weren't many signs of a meeting about to take place. We entered a dark, empty building, climbed a stairway, pushed open a half-panelled glass door at the top, and stepped into a thronged foyer. It wasn't very large, but all I could see were mothers, babies, and some young children. They quickly and quietly made way for us as we entered the main meeting hall. Grinning broadly, Fritz met us at the door, embraced us and, without speaking, beckoned us to follow him.

The building was full. Where had all these people come from, and how did they get here? I wondered. For the majority, it had meant a long journey on foot: some had walked for two hours to get to the meeting! It was a little easier for those who had access to a bus, tram, or bicycle.

We edged our way forward through the packed rows of seats, and sat down at the front beside a small platform and reading desk which supported two swan-necked microphones. There were seats on both sides facing the platform, with ladies on one side, and men on the other. This was the choir. Directly in front of us was a rather antiquated organ; beside it a cloth-covered table with some loaves, large jugs of wine and a number of empty glasses.

I was conscious that all eyes were on us. In the early 1980's visitors from the West were few and far between, so our presence was quite an experience for this congregation. I learned later that news of the resolution to the problem with the bus had spread around, and necks were stretched to see who had helped them in their time of need.

The meeting opened with the singing of a hymn - an enchanting melody in a minor key. The singing was strong, and the harmony moved me to tears. After an announcement, which I didn't understand, everybody got down on their knees to pray. This first prayer meeting in Romania is written deep on my heart. Many prayed. There were no pauses between the prayers. It seemed to me that there was a line-up to pray, and nobody wanted to miss out. Another contrast to home!

Generally speaking, in the large churches everyone was made welcome, although it was impossible for the leaders to know all who were present. They came in varied shapes, sizes, and forms of dress - just to be there, to hear the Word of God, was the important thing. Some of the Christians would invite their unconverted friends to come along.

On this occasion, the chairman for the day read 1 Corinthians chapter 11, and emphasised that only those who were washed in the blood of Christ could participate in breaking bread and drinking wine. Should they be unfit, and take the bread and wine, they would be *"guilty of the body and blood of the Lord Jesus"*.

After he had given thanks for the bread it was broken into small portions and put on to the plates, while he further explained the significance of the Lord's Death. As he did so, I noticed that the lapel of his coat was wet with tears. Then he gave thanks for the wine and it was poured out into the glasses. Because there were visiting speakers and such a large congregation, many of whom were standing, the bread and wine were distributed together, to save time.

My worship was stimulated by meditating on the Saviour's words, *"My body ... for you"*; and the teaching of the Apostle Paul, One bread, One body, One God, One Lord Jesus Christ, One Calvary, One common salvation.

We all sang another hymn, and the choir sang two pieces. I love singing, and this truly was heaven! Suddenly Gerald whispered to me, "They want you to sing a song for them. I told them you could sing and play the organ!". Before I could object, Fritz pointed to me and announced that I was going to sing. There was an excited movement all over the congregation. I was mortified! In normal circumstances I could have coped with this; but not that morning. However, I had no choice. Bewildered, I sat looking at the organ! How did it work? What buttons would I press? What should I sing?

Then I recalled a little hymn my father had written many years earlier, set to the famous Irish melody "The mountains of Mourne". Nervously, I began to sing:

In the Bible we read the sweet story of old,
Which to thousands on earth is more precious than gold!
It tells of a Saviour who came from above
To reveal to lost sinners God's wonderful love.
Was born in a manger, a Stranger was He;
Despised and rejected and nailed to the tree.
To put away sin, as the Lamb He was slain;
Then God raised and received Him to glory again.

And now, since He's risen and gone up on high,
He's preparing a home for His own in the sky.
And there in His Word, sure the promise is plain:
If I do go away, I will come back again.
Oh, why not believe this sweet story of old?
Then you will agree it's far better than gold,
To know sins forgiven, no judgment to dread -
Since Jesus the Saviour has died in your stead.

When I returned to my seat, everyone broke into muted, spontaneous applause. Many were smiling, some were weeping, despite the fact that they hadn't understood a word I had sung! It had to be translated so that they could get some idea of the message.

That is a very special memory to me still.

Incidentally, over the following days this little song became a MUST at every meeting. Word got round that the Irish preacher could sing! I'm just thankful that none of it was recorded! Singing it brought back a flood of memories of father's enjoyment of singing and playing; and how he, too, would have enjoyed being there.

When it was time for preaching, I spoke first. My translator was a dear, gentle man, called Ostavi. He spoke with a soft voice, in a non-demonstrative way.

I had been well warned to preach only the Word. Visiting speakers were discouraged from giving a resumé of their journey and, at all costs, to avoid public references to the congregation's disadvantaged conditions, or the state of the country. Any such reference could cause trouble later for the leaders, as it was quite common for informers to attend meetings. "Keep the message simple. Don't preach too fast. Make sure you give your translator proper sentences!" Gerald gave me these and other instructions while we were travelling.

Now the time had arrived, and I stood up to speak. To get my composure I looked around the audience, which I estimated to be about four hundred. Their eyes were twinkling, their faces beaming: they were eagerly anticipating a message from God's Word. I read the four references in the New Testament where it is recorded that *"Jesus was in the midst"*.

All went well until, in the middle of the message, I began to speak about Calvary and the saving work of the Lord Jesus, as He hung between the two malefactors. The translator suddenly stopped! I turned and looked at him. He was wiping away the tears, and stifling his sobs. I could do nothing. I just stood with my head bowed. In a few seconds he looked at me, smiled, and quietly said, "You can continue". But I had only spoken a few more sentences when he stopped again. He was sobbing; then I saw that everyone else was crying too. There was no embarrassment. The truth was, the Lord was there. He was 'in the midst', ministering to His suffering people.

Gerald then read the Scriptures, commented briefly on them, and followed with a graphic account of the famine in Ethiopia. He explained the great need of God's people in that land. "What can we do to help our brothers and sisters?", was the persistent question. Though they themselves had little of this world's goods, they realised only too well that the needs of the Christians in Ethiopia were much, much greater than theirs. I could not help thinking of the response of the impoverished Macedonian church, when the Apostle Paul told them of the great need of the churches in Judaea.

Looking back now, even after so many meetings and so many other marvellous experiences of the Lord's presence, this time has never been surpassed. In a temperature in the upper 20's C, the meeting lasted for four hours, followed by a further hour of handshakes, embraces and greetings. Over and over it came: *"Maranatha", "Maranatha", "Greetings in the name of the Lord Jesus Christ"*. We quickly understood this Romanian salutation.

A fitting postscript to an eventful first Breaking of Bread meeting, was the public confession of Jesus Christ as Saviour and Lord by some who had been invited to attend.

During the 1970's and 1980's, and in my experience right up to the present, it is normal to see people of all ages weep their way to the Saviour. Romania is a land of fiery evangelists. When they are released in the Spirit to preach, heaven comes near and hell is a reality. Like many other visiting speakers, I have had the privilege of seeing folk come to the Lord at the end of a message; but I soon realised that it didn't really matter who was preaching. The Holy Spirit was at work convicting and convincing of sin. People were marked out for salvation!

The evening service was in the town of Medias, thirty-five miles north of Sibiu. Five of us travelled inside an old, but well-maintained Dacia, with Fritz's extremely tall son folded up in the luggage compartment! On the return journey his wife pleaded to ride in style! When we arrived at their home, and opened up the boot, she was fast asleep! Her husband gently lifted her out and set her on her feet. She opened her eyes and beamed a radiant smile! I instinctively felt she had accomplished something special for the Lord.

It was all too much for me! I moved away a little distance so that I could have a good cry.

During that day's journey Fritz had explained to me that the last digit in a car's registration number was very important, as it was used as a method to ration fuel. Vehicles with odd numbers could travel on one Sunday, and those with even numbers could be used on the alternate Sundays. It was another, unbelievable, imposition put upon the hapless population.

That night in Room 109 I fell into a dreamless sleep. It had been quite a day!

CHAPTER VIII

Learning The Hard Way

As we drove down the seemingly endless German Auto bahn, Gerald had explained "Normally, we will have breakfast, and I would expect that later on in the evening we will get a meal in the home of one of the Christians".

"In between," he continued, "we will fast!"

This was a shock to my digestive system! For me, one of the interesting things about foreign travel is to sample the local restaurants and cafes. I explained to him light-heartedly that such long fasts from food didn't appeal to a Civil Servant, whose day would not be complete without the mandatory coffee and lunch breaks!

Gerald was amused. His face was a picture! "Restaurants? There aren't any eating places on the roads in Eastern Europe, and in Germany and Austria things are very expensive", he explained.

"Perhaps, occasionally, a can of coke and some crisps?" I pleaded!

"Drew", he said, "believe me: everything is very expensive. And, in any case, in Eastern Europe you need to be very careful about what you drink. The soft drinks are not proprietary brands; they are bottled locally, and you have no guarantee about hygiene."

We spent two nights in Hotel Continental in Sibiu, and then decided that we should try a different hotel. Hotel Bulevard was marginally better, and we could park the car in a less conspicuous place. All went well until we left Sibiu to travel south to Bucharest to deliver the, now lighter, school bag, and to contact the Christians. We approached the large city of Pitesti, the half-way mark. It was mid-day, and I was really hungry.

Breakfast in the Hotel Bulevard in Sibiu had been frugal: eggs, cheese and herb tea. I passed on the yoghurt, which Gerald really relished. As it was now several hours since then I enquired, tongue in cheek, about the possibility of a snack. But he was not for stopping! "There would be no suitable eating places here", he assured me.

"Just for today!" I persisted. "Surely we could find some place, somewhere?" Eventually he relented, probably out of embarrassment at my attitude. We turned into the main city area and found a car park, right beside a building displaying a large sign "RESTURANTI".

Once inside I realised I had made a big mistake, and was suddenly not very hungry at all! It was a dimly lit, dingy place, smelling strongly of beer. Groups of idle men, drinking their favourite brew, stopped to stare at us. We were different, very different! We found a table and asked for a menu.

"Sorry, no menu. We have soup and chicken", said the not too well turned-out waitress. Gerald ordered the soup. I said I would have the soup and the chicken. That was my second mistake! The soup was bordering on the obnoxious, and the chicken, when it came, was a plate full of burnt skin and bones, accompanied by very mushy potatoes and peas floating in a greenish gravy!

We struggled with the soup in silence, and Gerald solemnly watched as I tried to eat the chicken. He paid the bill and we left. For the second time on the trip I felt ashamed that I had been so persistent. I had done the very thing he warned me against, and I had wasted good money. The meal had cost the equivalent of five English pounds! Five pounds that could have helped someone in need! Shame turned to guilt, and I struggled once more with my conscience and stubborn will.

During the next two hours, as we travelled to Bucharest, I silently asked the Lord to help me curb my own wishes. I was not in charge of this mission, so I must try to do better from now on. My solemn thoughts were interrupted when Gerald said, "Do you notice anything different about this area?". To be honest, I hadn't been paying much attention to the scenery. Then I realised that we had left the mountains behind and were driving, mile after mile, through very flat agricultural land. "There are no poles or trees along the sides of the road. You will see that the surface is concrete, very straight and wide. It has a dual function: it serves as an airstrip, as well as the road! The President and his officials use it when they visit this area, and the military for their exercises, or emergencies", he explained.

That little conversation helped to ease the tension, and I knew that my companion was not holding anything against me. I wondered how I would have reacted, had the roles been reversed.

Next morning, when I awoke in the hotel in Bucharest, I had gastro-enteritis! I can vividly recall being on my knees in the bathroom, so very sick - and so very homesick! What was I going to do? From experience, I knew this could mean two or three days in bed with suitable medication. Then the guilt possessed me again. This was the price of my disobedience. The Lord was surely dealing with me, and I was proving to be a slow learner. All I could do was cry out to Him, ask His forgiveness, and plead that I would get sufficiently well to be able to continue the journey.

My immediate problem, though, was how to face Gerald!

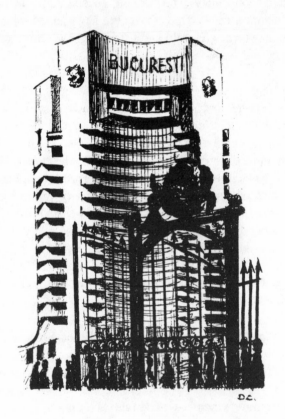

CHAPTER IX

The Impromptu Meeting

T he previous evening had been memorable. The foyer of the
Bucharest Intercontinental Hotel was an inhospitable place.
Some nondescript men stood, or sat, at vantage points,
surveying everything that moved. One felt eyes everywhere! We
had to make a telephone call to Lidia, and as discreetly as possible
get directions to her home.

After two abortive attempts, we finally contacted her. For three
days she had been waiting in her home for this call. Somehow, the
donor of the school bag had managed to get a telephone message
from Belfast. "A friend will call soon", she had been informed.

She gave us a tram number and details of where we should board
it. We already had the house number and street name. We quickly
returned to our rooms and filled two plastic bags with tinned food,
some other items, and, of course, the school bag. Ignoring the
persistent, gesticulating taxi drivers, we walked for one hundred
metres, made a right turn, and saw the tram-stop, with about fifty
people waiting. The street was very wide, with the tramlines in the

centre, and because it was the peak hour there was a lot of traffic moving up and down between the footpath and the trams.

"Keep close", called Gerald. "If the tram comes and we have to make a run for it, don't get separated."

Soon we saw it coming! With bulging bags in each hand, we rushed across, and happily got jammed on board in a tightly packed standing position. The tram jolted off and rattled along at some speed. We quickly realised that we could not see where we were going!

I said to Gerald, "You try to see out that side, and I'll try this side. We're looking for 131 Cal Plevnei."

After ten minutes or so (though it seemed much longer with the pressure building up inside us), the tram turned a corner and stopped, emptying sufficiently for me to get a look out. I caught a glimpse of the street nameplate. It was Cal Plevnei! I had the distinct feeling that the Lord was on our side!

"This is it now!" I almost shouted to Gerald, but he just nodded and said nothing. Earlier in the day we had stood out as foreigners, and the penny now dropped with me - we could be under surveillance. This was one of the many occasions when I was aware that we were not in a normal situation. It could be hostile territory; and, not least, we had to take into consideration that we might put at risk the people we were visiting.

We alighted at the correct place, right beside an army barracks, with a guard standing at the gate! As casually as possible, we crossed the street. Seemingly out of nowhere, a lady appeared, ushered us without ceremony through a gate, down a flight of stone steps into a basement apartment, and double bolted the door. Then she turned to face us with a radiant smile and a warm handshake. "You are welcome in the Name of the Lord Jesus Christ", she declared.

After exchanging greetings, meeting her husband and two children, we had a very welcome meal. What a contrast to our lunch stop in Pitesti! We handed over the gifts and the school bag, now safely arrived at its destination. When we told the story of what had happened at the frontier the children were all eyes and ears: this was a real adventure story!

After the meal, people began to arrive at the apartment in ones and twos, over a period of an hour. Lidia explained that these were some of the church leaders with their wives, whom she had contacted by coded message on the telephone. We were to have a time of fellowship.

We sang and prayed. It was real and intense prayer mixed with thanksgiving. Although I did not understand a word, there was a powerful communication in the Spirit. I did not feel in the least left out. What praise ascended to the risen Lord! There was an instant intimacy with heaven. Then, to my surprise, one or two prayed again in English. It must have been for our benefit.

We read the Scriptures together and Gerald and I were invited to bring a short message. It was during this that the door bell rang. The atmosphere changed from relaxation to tension. Lidia left the room. Our Romanian friends were praying silently. I was reminded of the situation at Fritz's home, and I wondered if the outcome would be as happy.

After some time Lidia returned, and signalled for her husband to join her. We remained in silence. Occasionally the Romanians would allow a fleeting smile to cross their lips. They were doing their best to make us feel at ease.

It was about half an hour before our hosts returned. They were smiling! Lidia informed us that it was her stepson who wanted to discuss something with them. He was not a believer, so they could not take any risks about what was going on in the house. They had talked as normally as they could in the kitchen. "In any case", she went on, obviously relieved, "he was in a hurry, so he left without any suspicion that a Christian meeting was taking place", (and two Westerners present, I thought).

The fellowship time came to an end with the singing of a Romanian hymn, followed by the benediction. Then we embraced, with unashamed tears and many "Maranathas". We were able to leave some financial help, and promised that we would try to assist them in buying a small car to help with the Lord's work in that part of the city.

Then as they had arrived so they left, singly or in small groups. They went out to the dark street, and disappeared into the night. Around midnight we caught the last tram into the city centre; and, being the only two passengers, we felt very uncomfortable.

That night, in my hotel bed, I closed my eyes and thanked the Lord for the unity of the Body of Christ. Until years later I didn't know that these dear folk were from a different church persuasion to mine. That one time we met, it was sufficient to know that we were one in Christ. Differences in doctrine, however important, could not extinguish the rich reality of kindred spirits under the control of the Holy Spirit.

Many years before, through much travail, the marvellous truth of the oneness of the Body of Christ had been born in my heart. It was now being reconfirmed and reinforced in another land and another culture. How I longed then, and still do, that the prayer of our Lord Jesus could find its practical fulfilment in our generation: *"That they may be one, as we are"* (John 17:11) .

CHAPTER X

Joy In Shared Tears

"You look ill", Gerald observed, when I joined him, as an embarrassed spectator, at the breakfast table. I explained that I felt very ill, and didn't know if I would be able to continue. At the table he committed the situation to the Lord. There were no recriminations, just real sympathy. Once in the car, he prayed again and asked the Lord for help in this unexpected situation. He tried to console me by telling me that the journey to Brasov was not too long.

I slept most of the way, and four hours later I was tucked up in bed in the Hotel Capital. The hotel was overshadowed by the mountains. Their beauty was accentuated by a cloudless sky and brilliant sunshine, but all this had no appeal for me at that moment!

Before leaving, Gerald told me that he was going to locate his friends so that they could arrange a meeting in the church. "It usually begins about six o'clock, but I will come back for you before then, and see how you are." As far as his friends were concerned, this would be another visit of 'angels from heaven', and I was determined, if at all possible, to be at the meeting. Thankfully, I slept.

I awoke with a loud banging at the door. I jumped out of bed. My head spun and I was again violently sick. But I managed to communicate to Gerald that I would be ready in ten minutes. As I washed and dressed, I really prayed that the Lord would help me to go through with the evening, and I did feel a little better when I met him in the hotel foyer.

Without asking how I was feeling, he urged "We must hurry! My friend is waiting in his car across the road. I will go over and get in. He will drive up to the end of the street, turn and come down again. When he stops, please get in quickly." I did so, and found myself staring at a somewhat startled young man with spectacles, who greeted me briefly, with the faint sign of a smile. Then he drove off at speed to the meeting.

It was not a large building, but it was very full. We were ushered up to the front seat and the service commenced with the usual prayer time, followed by singing. I began to feel ill, so I enquired through Gerald if there was a toilet in the building. After a brief discussion with the man beside me, he said that if I needed to leave he would come with me and show me where to go.

Gerald proposed that, because of my discomfort, I should just give a greeting from the Scriptures, and I readily agreed. So when my turn came we both moved on to the small platform. As this was a German-speaking church, he would translate for me. I announced the Scripure reading and began to read, when suddenly I felt very ill. I knew I had to leave immediately. I rushed to the door, opened it, and in my haste I missed my footing on the steps and landed in a heap on the concrete floor! In retrospect, I have often wondered what the congregation thought was happening!

"A cup of cold water in my Name": the words floated around in my head as I emerged from another bout of sickness. My friend, who had followed me, now had a glass of water in his hand. As I drank it thankfully, he reached me a handkerchief, and putting his

arm on my shoulder he squeezed it tight. His eyes were moist. We went back into the hall, but I took no further part. Gerald had explained to the audience that "the brother" was not feeling well. I was very happy just to be able to sit through to the end without causing any further disturbance!

We went to the home of our new friend's mother. I ate no food. After sharing some gifts we prepared to depart. Just as we were leaving, the lady of the house - a dear, gentle person - asked me to take a little medicine which she had prepared. I took it gladly, though it was not at all pleasant to swallow. Together with her very large family, we prayed for healing.

What a relief it was, when I finally crawled into bed. Once more, from the safety of the sheets, I asked the Lord for his urgent help. I closed my eyes and slept soundly. Next morning when I awoke the sun was shining brilliantly. Better still, I felt as though I had never been ill!

It was as close to a miracle as I had ever experienced. I was learning in the school of discipleship, and realising more and more that in this society there was plenty of room for the Lord to work. Dependence on Him, from hour to hour, was the normal way of life for these Romanian Christians. They had an uncomplicated belief in the Lord, particularly in relation to the things that I might have deemed coincidental.

It was a far cry from the mechanical experience that characterises Christian life at home. Most things are taken care of, arranged or rearranged, with little recourse to prayer. We don't seem to feel the need of Divine intervention. Two completely different ways of life. Like Mary of Bethany, I knew who had the *"better part"*.

CHAPTER XI

The Czechoslovakian Experience

O n Thursday 10th September 1987 I travelled by air from Belfast to Vienna en route to Eastern Europe for the second time. The plan was to meet up with Gerald there and spend time with Roberta Stevenson and other staff members at the Child Evangelism Fellowship Headquarters.

Roberta originated from my home church at Brooklands, Dundonald. She had been commended by our fellowship to the Lord's work in Eastern Europe, and was then making frequent covert journeys behind the Iron Curtain. There she met with small groups of Christians who were secretly teaching the gospel to children, and needed Bible teaching material.

The story of CEF's operations during many difficult years in Eastern Europe should one day be fully told. I have no doubt that heaven has taken note of those pioneers who, in difficult and lonely situations, helped to equip the Christians to spread the good news of the gospel among the Eastern European children. They will have their reward from the best of Masters.

I rushed my trolley through the Customs' green channel. Piled into a pyramid shape were three cases, two bags, and two cardboard cartons, plus hand luggage!

"Nothing to declare?", a curious, uniformed customs lady enquired.

"This is for humanitarian relief in Czechoslovakia and Romania", I replied.

"You certainly must know a lot of people!", she remarked, as she smiled and waved me through.

The reception party was waiting at the barrier. Gerald, tousled-haired, and beaming; Roberta, excitement written all over her face; and her CEF colleague, Eric, with whom we were to stay overnight. We exchanged greetings, and then from Gerald: "Drew! Where do you think we're going to put all this baggage? I left some space for your luggage, but not for this mountain!"

It was a familiar problem. No matter how methodically the cases were packed, nor how selective I tried to be, there never seemed to be sufficient room for what I considered necessary. I never deliberately concealed anything in my luggage. I was not aware of any written regulations setting out what we could, and could not, take. My mission was not one of beating the Customs or the Secret Police; but it was very obvious that decisions were made on-the-spot, by greedy-eyed and corrupt Frontier officials. Over many years these people feathered their nests and lined their pockets with things they had no right to have.

After an overnight of fellowship in Vienna we set about re-packing Gerald's vehicle. Regrettably, we did have to leave some things behind. Our host said he would take them on a future visit to Romania. So we said our good-byes and headed north to the Czechoslovakian border, near Bratislava.

Getting through Customs and Security was not too difficult, taking less than an hour. We travelled on to Brno, arriving at 7.00 p.m., booked into a hotel, and decided not to make contact with the Christians until the next morning, which was Saturday. As it happened, on that particular Saturday the thrice-yearly meeting of the "Council of Brethren Churches" in C.S.S.R. was being convened. This was an all-day administration meeting, with a time set aside for prayer. These meetings were required by law. All the details and arrangements for church gatherings, speakers, etc., for the following three months, were agreed in detail, and the information submitted to the Authorities.

We tried to contact the person we had been with in 1984. His wife informed us that he was "at the church", but she would send a message to him. In the mid morning, he joined us at the home of another Christian known to Gerald and, after discreet but warm greetings, he thought a little about what it would be best to do.

He decided that I could attend the meeting after lunch, as an interested friend travelling through Eastern Europe. However, it would be inadvisable for me to participate in any way, as the Authorities might have a representative present, or they could drop in without prior warning. He then left and, as promised, returned at about 1.30 p.m.

We travelled to the venue at some speed over the rough, cobbled city streets and tramlines in his 1969 Skoda! I could not help thinking of Nehemiah's comment *"the King's business requires haste"*! I was amazed at the pristine condition of this eighteen year old car. It was obviously his pride and joy.

This was only one of many fast and furious vintage car journeys in those years in Eastern Europe.

When I entered the local church building, where the Council meeting was being convened, I found about forty elderly and middle-aged men sitting at tables, in groups of five or six. I was shown to a seat beside a man who spoke a little English and who, in loud whispers, kept me informed of the proceedings.

At the conclusion of the main agenda, under Any Other Business, there was an opportunity for open discussion. It seemed to me that it was "getting-it-all-off-the-chest" time! Local problems, clarification-seeking, and a number of doctrinal questions that appeared to be causing confusion and difficulty in some of the churches, were vigorously debated.

Some people had travelled a distance, and obviously wanted the proceedings to end; but like so many open-ended discussions there seemed to be no end! The interjections were many and urgent, at least to those whose particular problem was under consideration.

The meeting eventually concluded, with the brethren on their knees, one after the other, commending the activities, arrangements and discussions to the Lord. After the prayer time I was informally introduced to some of the "leading men". They were polite, but very reserved, and I wondered if my visit at this particular gathering had caused embarrassment. However, I was assured that this was not the case. Their demeanour ensued from the many years of being under surveillance and oppression. They were not free men, and I had to learn to appreciate this.

I arranged with my 'chauffeur' that he would collect me at our hotel at 8.30 a.m. the next morning, Sunday, to go to the Breaking of Bread service. Gerald had been invited by his friend to participate in another service in a different part of the city.

In my room I again contemplated the closed society that Marxism had inflicted upon the Christians, and how, undeterred, they still pursued the traditions of their fathers in upholding God's Word and their right to meet together in fellowship to worship the Lord and proclaim the gospel of Christ. This was a situation which required them to live in the present possession of fellowship with the Lord, taking their direction from Him. Superficial Christianity would not survive long in such a climate.

Next morning, prompt at 8.30, I was collected by my friend Peter, and we returned to the church in the Skoda. I complimented him about the car, commenting on its immaculate condition, showing no signs of wear and tear. He told me how glad he was to have it, and continued "We have many brothers who cannot properly do God's work because they do not have this means of travel. Our congregation is very scattered. Some people live in isolated places and it is really difficult for our elders to visit them."

The service was divided into three elements. The first thirty minutes was given to prayer; the next to praise and breaking of bread. I was then invited to speak. "Take about fifteen minutes", Peter said. "Feel free to read the Scriptures and bring greetings." The meeting concluded with ministry from a local brother.

I was entertained to lunch at Peter's home. Afterwards we went to a village about twenty miles from Brno for an afternoon gospel meeting. This was a small assembly, meeting in very primitive circumstances in a room in a farm house.

It was extremely hot, which made preaching by interpretation very trying. The meeting could have lasted indefinitely. I found playing and singing at their antiquated pedal organ hard work, but they loved it! It was surprising how many of their hymn tunes we knew, but when we compared the words they were usually altered or completely different. The expressions of sheer delight on their faces, and the enthusiasm of their participation, made me realise how real was their devotion to the Lord, and how greatly they valued fellowship with other Christians.

When, finally, we managed to finish, a space was cleared and a table spread for food. My lasting memory of the surroundings is of rows of rabbit pelts, hanging on hooks around the room. These folk lived very close to the ground!

We returned to our host's home and had one hour for 're-charging our batteries'. It was at this time that I discovered in a book case, a book entitled "Shepherd of Lonely Sheep" by James Lees, the Scottish miner, who in the early part of this century became a missionary and travelled in uncomfortable and hazardous conditions through Europe, preaching the Word and tending to the flock of God.

It was a poignant moment for me because I remembered as a child meeting Mr. Lees in our home.

Before leaving the next morning I had read the whole book! I was humbled before the Lord as, in spirit, I followed the travels, trials and triumphs of this honoured servant of God. However difficult the present political situation was, we were travelling and living in luxury, compared to the experiences of this pioneer of the gospel.

After some light refreshment we returned to the evening service, which was attended by about one hundred people. Gerald had joined us again, and we were allocated twenty minutes each.

"You can read from the Scriptures and bring a gospel message, but do not refer to conditions here, or where you intend to travel in Eastern Europe. We do not know who might be present", we were informed. There was only one message I could bring. It was *"The good Shepherd giveth his life for the sheep"*, from John ch. 10. The Word of God came that evening with softness and extraordinary power.

We fully intended to return to our hotel, as required by law; but yielded to pressure from our hosts to stay overnight in their home, when we were assured that this would not cause any difficulty. It had been another long, but happy, day. We had made new friends, and the link that binds believers in the Body life of the church had been strengthened.

We returned to Vienna by lunch time the next day, Monday, and drove on through Budapest to a small town near the Hungarian-Romanian border. We arrived at 11.00 p.m. and found meagre but adequate accommodation.

D.C.

CHAPTER XII

Under Surveillance

"**D**o you have any Bibles?", the question came to us at the
Romanian frontier. It was April 1987. We had been there
for one hour and, as in the 1984 visit, our passports had
been taken from us.

I was startled by its directness. Gerald replied, "Yes, we have",
and he paused before adding, "our own personal copies!". The car
was totally ransacked but, without any further inquisition, we were
allowed to pass through. The whole operation had been completed
in a little over two hours. As usual, we had committed the crossing
to the Lord, asking for His protection and help. Now we rejoiced
together that we were once again on Romanian soil.

Before resuming our journey we discussed the question about
the Bibles. We came to the conclusion that their computer records
had us accurately assessed: we were 'tourists' of a special kind!
"It means", said Gerald, "that they know that we are not normal
tourists, and we will most probably be closely watched; but we're
in the Lord's hands. I am always more concerned about the effect
that visits like these have for the Christians here than for myself."

It was dark by the time we entered the Bulevard Hotel in Sibiu city centre. We filled in the registration forms, changed some money, and bought petrol coupons. The routine was becoming familiar. We then went to Fritz's home, but there was no one there. Everything was in total darkness, no vehicles on the streets, no noise.

We waited for about fifteen minutes, wondering what we should do. Occasionally someone would shuffle past our car, and we could see them stare at it and try to see the registration plate. Before the Revolution Western cars were objects of curiosity. It was uncomfortable, and not a little eerie.

Gerald decided that we would abandon the visit until the morning, and we were just about to go when someone in an old Dacia car arrived at the house. The driver got out, paused, and looked in our direction, and then pressed the bell on the high, green wooden gate. He soon realised that there was no one there, and returned to his car. He hesitated again, as he very deliberately looked over in our direction.

Gerald said "I wonder if he is a member of the church". Then, without pausing, he continued, "I think I recognise him", and with that he got out and walked to where he was, and they talked together for a few minutes.

When he returned, he confirmed that his hunch had been correct. He was a friend, and suggested that it was possible that the family were at a choir practice in the church. He told Gerald to follow him, and he would guide us there. "I think I know the way", Gerald told him, but he insisted that we follow him.

We had a quick, rough and tense journey. Trying to keep his car in sight was an art in concentration. We went through NO ENTRY signs, negotiated massive holes and high, hardened, mud ruts! Now to the left, through an arch, down a steep hill, along narrow, unlit streets. It was a nightmare! Finally, with a flutter in my heart,

I recognised the old factory building where we had enjoyed such precious fellowship three years before. Our guide's assumption proved to be correct. We climbed the stairs, and unceremoniously interrupted the choir practice.

'The angels from heaven' had descended once again!

A wonderful, tearful reunion followed. The Romanians couldn't take it in that we were really there! Needless to say, our arrival spoiled the choir practice; but they were all overcome with joy. There would be plenty of other times to practise without interruption - at least of a friendly kind!

We returned to Fritz's house, had some strong coffee and little cakes baked by the ever-smiling Letitia. She was no longer restrained and, listening to her hearty laugh, it was difficult to believe that, in common with other Christians in Sibiu at that particular time, they were experiencing unprecedented pressure from the Authorities. No definite alternative had yet been found for the new church building, and the final ultimatum had been given.

Fritz was a master craftsman, a cabinet-maker by trade. Because of the good relationship with his manager, he was able to get unpaid leave to be with us. We decided on our programme for the next five days, handed over some gifts and finance for the new building, and prayed together. I still could not understand German, but Gerald translated their prayers for me. As I prayed, I felt the firm grip of Fritz's hand around my shoulder, and I knew by the clearing of his throat and the stifled sobs that he was weeping: not with sorrow for their afflictions, but with sheer joy at our reunion, and the anticipation of a few days of fellowship together. To him, this was a foretaste of heaven!

Soon we were back at the hotel, happy that our mission to bring comfort, cheer and the Word of God to these beleaguered Christians had begun in earnest. What we didn't know was that the Secret Police were monitoring our movements.

This became very apparent the next morning, when we rendez-voused with Fritz and Costica Morariu in the hotel car park. The soft-hatted men were about! All of the day was taken up, buying food in bulk at the Comturist Duty-free shop in Sibiu's main street. Goods in this store were available only to those trading in foreign currency. We also spent several hours in a bank trying to transfer money for the purchase of a vehicle for church work.

The day was not only one of activity and frustration, but one of intense prayer. It was obvious to us that the two Romanians were feeling the strain. When all was accomplished, we retired for a wash and change of clothing; and then we made our way to a village about thirty-five miles from Sibiu for an impromptu meeting.

The 'carrier pigeon' system had been in operation earlier in the day. The news was conveyed to the village that brothers from the West would be visiting that evening to preach the Word of God, and the Christians should gather at 6.30 p.m.

They did!

The building was too small. All the backless seats were occupied, and there was standing room only. They came as they were, from the fields and the factories. Their joy was undimin-ished. The congregation was divided in the middle by a centre aisle, with the women to the left and the men to the right, looking from front to back, as is the Romanian custom. The front three or four rows were occupied by dark-eyed children, who enjoyed the service with the same intensity as their parents. Over and over, we had translated to us "We are glad that you have not forgotten us!".

The stanza of a hymn from our worship hymnbook very often comes to mind on these occasions:

Oh, if this glimpse of love
Is so divinely sweet,
What will it be, Oh Lord, above,
Thy gladdening smile to meet!

To see Thee face to face,
Thy perfect likeness wear;
And all Thy ways of wondrous grace
Through endless years declare.

Before we preached the Word, we had the wonderful privilege of listening to the Iach (pronounced Yak) family play and sing. This is perhaps one of the best known families among Brethren churches in Transylvania. All visitors to their home in Cisnadie are serenaded with gospel music and song, as they dine in their home after the services. That evening, in that remote mountain village, we had blessing in salvation, and the Christians were overjoyed. We said our farewells amid more embraces and the familiar "Maranathas". How different it all was to church life at home.

The Scriptures speak of *"blackness of darkness"*. I was reminded of this when we stumbled out into the pitch black, deeply rutted and extremely muddy village street. Very quickly, flash lamps were stabbing their points of light and guiding all concerned on their happy way. It never occurred to me that the Securitate would be interested in us at this time of night; but we learned later that we had been followed, waited for, and pursued to the hotel. On some occasions they would be sitting in the hotel lobby, ready to exchange pleasantries with us!

"Did you have a good day today, gentlemen?", the question delivered in perfect English from a smiling face. In these encounters we did not fear for ourselves, but kept wondering what trouble was storing up for those brave enough to expose themselves to our friendship.

The following Sunday morning, it was decided that we would share in two Breaking of Bread meetings. We would travel eight miles south to Cisnadie for the first part of their service, and then return to the Sibiu meeting for the latter part of theirs; so we were collected at the hotel by Marianne Iach at 7.00 a.m. She took us to their home for breakfast, then on to the meeting.

From the time we were collected at the hotel until we arrived at the church, unknown to us, we were being trailed by the Securitate. Marianne spotted them, but said nothing. They knew the Cisnadie service finished around 12.00 noon, so when they returned at that time they found that the Westerners had vanished! The Cisnadie folk got quite a bit of amusement out of seeing the frustrated police combing the streets and picking out houses of prominent Christians in an effort to find us.

We travelled to a village in the mountains for the evening service, only to find that our 'friends' had arrived before us! Unabashed, they parked their vehicle on the corner of the street beside the meeting house. How did they know we were going to this particular village?

We never did find the answer!

CHAPTER XIII

A Romanian Martyr

O n a visit to the Iach family in Cisnadie I met their niece, a young widow called Nina Teodosiu, and her seven year old son, Eldad. Her husband Sabin had been killed in 1982. The circumstances surrounding his death were very suspicious. The family were soon convinced that he had been killed on the orders of the Securitate.

Nina told me the story of her husband's love for the Lord, and his remarkable gift for evangelism, which had been obvious even before they were married.

Sabin had a love for the elderly and the sick, and would often visit them to bring the gospel. He was a member of the Sibiu Baptist church. Prior to their marriage he started to visit small churches. Every week he travelled to help some of them, always carrying a bag full of books and Bibles.

He was employed in the High Voltage line section of the Electricity Company. It was a dangerous occupation. All the employees were required to sign a paper each month, acknowledging that they were prepared to do this type of work.

Nina and he met at youth meetings, and were married in 1980. Sabin's burden for preaching the gospel increased, and he began preaching every night as well as at week-ends. He travelled by bus or train, and sometimes he walked.

There was one special area of work in a village called Giulesti. To be there for meeting time on Sunday morning, it meant travelling all night - about one hundred miles by train, followed by a ten mile walk. Sabin would stay there all day, preaching and teaching, and return overnight by train ready for work on Monday morning.

Sometimes Christian friends would take him by car, but mostly the cost of his travel was taken from his salary.

The church began to grow.

In another church, in the village of Vurpar, many people were saved. Sabin publicly distributed tracts and told people about salvation. This soon brought him into conflict with the authorities. One Friday in March 1981 he and four others were on their way to a church when a tyre burst, and they crashed the car. They all received minor injuries and the Police took them to hospital. When the doctors had finished treating Sabin, he gave them gospel tracts.

At this time Nina was expecting a baby. On the Monday after the accident when Sabin came home, he said to her, "Maybe it is better just to have our own copies of the Bible and books. We should put the others in a safe place". Nina told me, "He did not want to worry me, but I knew there was something happening so I asked him what was going on".

He said, "When we were at the hospital on Friday night, I gave some tracts to a lady doctor. She went to the Securitate, and I have been told to expect a visit from them! We decided to commit this situation to the Lord and do nothing for some days, until we would see if the visit would happen", Nina continued.

No one came.

After a while Sabin continued on as before with his work for the Lord. On the Sunday before he died, he and some friends from Cisnadie visited five churches, covering a distance of sixty miles. They left before 7.00 o'clock in the morning, and did not return until about 9.00 o'clock that evening.

The following Tuesday he went to work. He usually returned about 3.00 o'clock, but he never came home.

"When did you begin to get worried?", I asked Nina.

"Normally", she replied, "when Sabin went to work, I would take Eldad, who was then two months old, for a walk, and I usually called in to see my friends in a shop where I used to work. Eldad was a very good baby, and very seldom cried. That day, at about 12.00 o'clock, we were in the shop, and he began to cry very loudly, for no apparent reason. I could not understand why he was so distressed, as he had been fed and changed. I thought he must have pain."

"Did he cry for long?"

"For about fifteen minutes! I could not get him to be quiet. I took him home and put him to bed."

"At 3.55 p.m. Sabin's two brothers came to my mother's house to tell her that Sabin was dead. My mother came and told me. I was stunned!"

Nina then explained to me the circumstances which they had pieced together over the following days, as they tried to find out what had happened.

A Christian friend from the church, who knew him very well, worked at the hospital. As she passed through the mortuary she saw Sabin. She was shocked, and immediately went to find one of his brothers to tell him what she had discovered. Later that day his two brothers went to the Electricity Station to ask what had happened. They discovered some interesting things.

"On the Tuesday morning," Nina explained, "when Sabin went to get his working instructions for the day, he was asked by his boss to sign one of the 'danger papers'. As I told you, this normally happened only once a month, and each of his colleagues had to sign it. That morning Sabin was the only one who was asked. They said it was a special job. The job was to make some repairs on a 110 kv tower. His boss and a colleague went with him in the van. When they arrived at the place, the power was disconnected and Sabin climbed the tower to do the repair work. His boss and the colleague remained on the ground about twelve metres away."

"It was normal for the person on the tower to get back to the ground before the electricity was reconnected, but while Sabin was still on the tower the power came on and he was immediately electrocuted. He was thrown to the ground, and died instantaneously. It was 12.00 - the time Eldad began to cry in the shop!"

Sabin's brothers persisted with questions. Why? How could this happen? But there was no answer. It was an accident!

In the station Sabin had a very good colleague, a German. When he was asked what happened, he said "Look, I want to go to Germany, and if I tell you they will stop me from going. Maybe one day I can tell you what happened."

"Did he go to Germany?" I enquired.

"Yes, he did. But we decided not to ask him any questions."

"Was there an inquest?" I asked.

"No, there was nothing like that. Usually, when something serious happened, the boss would be held responsible; but in this case, at the end of the year, the boss was promoted! We thought about going to an advocate to pursue the matter, but we were told it would just be a waste of time."

I then asked Nina how she had been sustained over the years. She said her faith in God had become more real. Her family had rallied round to help her, and she was happy now that she was involved full time in the Lord's work with children.

"In what way?", I asked.

"With Child Evangelism Fellowship" she said, smiling. "I help with administration in the C.E.F. office in Sibiu."

It's a small world, I thought. Back in 1990, the idea that a house should be purchased and used as a CEF centre in Romania was conceived in the mind of Roberta Stevenson, the European Co-ordinator for Child Evangelism Fellowship in Romania. Roberta is a very dear friend. I had known her from her early teens, when she attended our church in Dundonald. The Lord had led her to Switzerland to train to be a teacher of teachers working with children in Eastern Europe. Before the Revolution she travelled incognito under the name of "Joy", and at considerable risk had established good contacts. Now that freedom had come, she felt it was time to establish a permanent CEF centre in Romania, and chose Sibiu in the centre of the country. In unusual circumstances, obviously guided by the Lord, she purchased the house where Nina now works!

Such are the ways of our God. How true it is, *"He doeth great things past finding out; yea, and wonders without number"* (Job 9:10).

This Romanian martyr must surely be only one of an uncountable number who, in our modern world, have laid down their lives for the cause of the Master they loved to serve.

The old adage is still true, "The blood of the martyrs is the seed of the church".

CHAPTER XIV

Undercover Transportation

I learned from Mircea Cioâta, a leading elder in the large Brethren church in Ploiesti, that, from the inception of Communism in 1944 until 1970, the Government had a law which permitted humanitarian help to come into Romania, without being taxed. During these years much help came from Western Europe, particularly from Germany.

Many German Romanians lived in Northern Transylvania - in Cluj, Sibiu, Sighisoara, Brasov, and other large cities. There was a significant traffic in Western vehicles bringing in aid, and along with this aid came many Bibles and all sorts of Christian literature. This was done secretly; many accounts have been written, detailing how this was accomplished. And not only to Romania, but to many of the Eastern Bloc countries.

At the same time, in the South of Romania, the River Danube - the large waterway that marked the boundary between Romania and its neighbours, Bulgaria and Yugoslavia - was used as an artery for the undercover transportation of Bibles and Christian books. However, in contrast to the North of the country, there were no

German Romanians living in the South. All the cars, vans, etc. were Romanian, and their movements were easier to watch.

A city in Transylvania, approximately in the centre of Romania, was used by the Brethren churches as the underground headquarters for the collection and distribution of the Bibles.

At first they concentrated on the supplies coming overland from Germany, the Netherlands, and as far west as England. Then, when the "Danube Run" began, the main concentration of activity was switched to the South.

Over a period of four years, one particular ship carried four consignments of twenty thousand Bibles to a specified "safe" dock. Audio equipment, watches, food, and other contraband were also brought in by this method. This harbour was selected because it was near to a forest. The time of the ship's arrival was communicated through the German network to those trusted Christians who had agreed to travel South to collect and distribute the Bibles.

Usually they used ten to twelve cars, and for one consignment it would take many runs to the ship, spread over three or four nights. All the road approaches to the forest had Police checkpoints. The Authorities were alert to the possibility of contraband being smuggled from the ships to the shore. However, the Danube border was very long and dotted with many small ports where ships stopped to load and unload cargo in the normal way. The Police activity was, therefore, spread out over a very large area of country.

They used the Book of Proverbs as a code for the dates and times of the ship's arrival. There are thirty-one chapters; the chapter number was the day of the month, and the verse number was the time of the day! The cars, with two people in each - taking it in turns to drive and rest - would converge on the forest, from all angles and at different times.

The journeys were difficult and dangerous. They would use byways, unmarked tracks, rough ground, and then park the cars as close as possible to the river. If there was a Police checkpoint nearby, they would drive without lights, and switch off their engines when going down slopes in the forest.

When all the vehicles were in place, at a pre-arranged time they would walk to the ship. Everything was very still, and it was possible to move in under the cover of darkness and carry the boxes of books and Bibles from the ship.

On one particular ship the Captain, who was not a Christian, was willing to bring the Bibles. He was paid for this. Mircea continued, "We were able to receive the boxes from him, and carry them back to the cars, filling up the boot and the floor at the back. On the first journey we drove to a mill which was owned by a Christian. We unloaded all the boxes, storing them in the roof of the mill. Over the following weeks, they were collected by people whom we didn't know, and distributed in the Southern part of the country."

"Our second load from the ship was taken North for distribution in villages in each of our areas. Trusted friends took the boxes into their homes, outhouses, or other secure places."

"All of this was accomplished by working hard throughout the night, and we went straight to our jobs in the morning."

"When the ship arrived, we worked as usual until about three o'clock in the afternoon and then made our way, by different routes, to the forest or nearest town. We would start at about six o'clock, when it was dark, and work throughout the night. Before daylight broke we would suspend operations until the next night."

"Were you ever stopped or questioned?", I asked.

"Not me personally," he said. "But one night we were on a main road near a checkpoint, when the car in front of mine had a burst tyre. I didn't know what had happened, and thought they had been stopped by the Police. I quickly turned round and drove off in another direction, but we were not familiar with the road and got completely lost! Sometimes it was really very difficult."

"There was another occasion, when my brother Silviu was the passenger in the back of the car. A Policeman waved me to stop, and he asked me for a lift! I said 'Da, Da' (Yes, Yes), trying to keep my composure. My brother is not very tall, and he was sitting low in the back seat, so in the dark the Policeman did not see him! We were stopped at a checkpoint in a town, but the Policeman said 'I am in a big hurry. It's all right!' - and we were allowed to drive through."

"Did you have any Bibles in the car at the time?" I asked him.

"Da, Da - it was full! When he arrived at his destination he thanked me for helping him and got out, still without noticing my brother! You can understand our great relief!"

Many Christian groups were involved in collecting the Bibles from the "safe houses". Baptists, Pentecostals, even Adventists asked if they could have Bibles! All went well until October 1981, when the 'team' knew that something was wrong. News came through from Germany that the contact for the ship had been arrested and under questioning by the Securitate he had confessed to bringing in contraband, including Bibles. Under severe pressure he eventually gave eleven names of those he knew to be involved. This led to their arrest, trial and imprisonment.

CHAPTER XV

The Test Of Faith

Mircea's wife, Flori, continued the story of the events as they unfolded over the next days, weeks and months. "Of the eleven implicated by the ship's contact, nine were men and two were young women in their mid-twenties. These were hard times, not only for the immediate families, but for everyone involved in the 'safe houses' in the various villages. News spread quickly about the possibility of searches, and there was great fear throughout the Christian communities."

"At 5.45 one morning, before Mircea went to his work, our door bell rang. I opened the door. There was a uniformed Policeman and two others whom I took to be Securitate. They said they had reason to believe that we had contraband goods in the house, and they had come to search. No one was allowed to leave and no telephone calls could be taken or made. Our three children couldn't go to school or college."

"They searched until one o'clock."

"My husband had open bookshelves in two rooms. They took out all the books and went through each one, piling them on the floor in the middle of the room. I knew they were looking for foreign currency, or anything that would incriminate us."

"Did they find anything?" I asked.

"No. Nothing! They searched our kitchen, looking for tins or jars with foreign labels; but they didn't find any. We were very apprehensive because we had two secure places in the apartment where we had many boxes of Bibles, but they would have had to break down the furniture to find them and they did not do this."

"They also looked for technical books to do with our work, as it was illegal to remove these from the work place."

"All the time we were casting glances of comfort and assurance to each other and silently committing the situation to the Lord. We knew He was in control and we must trust Him."

"They wrote down details of everything, and when they were finished they asked my husband to accompany them to the office to make a declaration about what they had found. He was questioned and kept in the Securitate basement all night, and released the next day. Over the following weeks he was called regularly from his job and from home, to make further declarations."

"There was no destruction of our belongings, but it took us a week to sort out the terrible mess and get the house back in order."

Mircea took up the story: "As part of my work, as a member of the Institute of Oil Drilling Engineers, I travelled to other countries to advise on oil drilling operations. In January 1982 I was sent for three months to Russia."

"Two days after returning home a car stopped beside me on the street, and I was told to get in. I was taken to the Securitate office and questioned for some hours. They put me into the basement, and for the next week I was interrogated by many different officers.

"Did they physically abuse you?" I asked him.

"Yes", he replied. "Because I was very calm and patient in my answers they became very angry. This led to some violence, and I ended up with minor bruising."

"What was this basement like?", I queried.

"It was just a small room, all of concrete, two concrete slabs for beds and a hole in the floor for a toilet. During the daytime we had to stand against the wall, and only at night were we allowed to lie down on the concrete beds."

Flori continued her story: "When my husband did not come home I had an idea that he might be with the Securitate; but on the other hand, he might have had an accident. What was happening to my husband was also happening to all the others, but our families weren't told what was going on. We kept in touch with each other, and our trust was in God."

"A trial in 'open' court took place without the families knowing about it. By law the hearing had to be in public, but they filled the court with Securitate, their friends, and officials - everybody but the families concerned. Eventually my niece received word through a friend that nine of them had been sentenced to five years and four months. Silviu, his brother, and another friend, Costel, were each given a six year sentence."

"This cannot be true", I protested. "We have heard of no court case; we have had no news of any kind. It cannot be true!"

"One of the wives went to the Securitate office with warm clothes for her husband. They spoke to her very harshly: "How do you know he is here? He is not here!", they said.

"Eventually, through the Court Secretary - the wife of an Engineer friend of my husband - we found out that it was true. It was a great shock, and a time of severe testing for all the families involved. Because it was a 'political' trial, there were no records, no newspaper reports - nothing. Just silence!"

"The families decided that they must make an appeal, and we tried to hire an advocate. This proved exceedingly difficult, as it was not a normal advocacy situation and everyone was afraid to speak out against the State. However, after some time we managed to find one who agreed to lodge an appeal."

"Maybe" he said, "it will take one or two weeks before it will happen."

"We paid for the appeal at 9.30 one morning, and at two o'clock the same day the court sat! There was no change in the verdict. It was a sham, just a waste of time and money."

Flori continued, "Unknown to us, they were held for some time in the Securitate basements, but eventually they were taken two by two in handcuffs to a prison about twenty miles north of Ploiesti. Due to the fact that there were no records of the arrests, charges, trial, or appeal, they were put in a special part of the prison and treated differently from the other prisoners."

"We visited the Securitate office many times during the next few weeks, asking Why? and Where?; and eventually we got to find out where they were and were able to make arrangements to visit them. Each time we went we took five kilos of food."

"After three months Mircea lost his job. They said he was condemned because he tried to destroy the State, but this could not have been further from the truth. It was well known by those in authority in work places, that the Christians were the best and most honest workers for their country."

Due to the "Most Favoured Nation" status, Romania received from the United States of America special trading concessions and additional finance. Because President Ceaucescu, in his early days in office, had taken an independent line from the Soviet Bloc and the Warsaw Pact countries, he was honoured by the United Kingdom government. Generally, therefore, Romania was looked upon with favour by Western nations. The quid pro quo for this was that the Romanian government would grant to all its citizens religious and political freedom. For some time these freedoms were violated, and when news of the arrests, trial and imprisonment of the eleven dissidents leaked out, the United States government made representation to the Romanian government. Questions were asked. Diplomatic interaction was intense; and eventually, on 29th July 1982, all the prisoners were released except one. He had been taken to a prison in Bucharest, but was released the following day, 30th July.

Flori concludes the story: "On 29th July I received a telephone call from Mircea. 'Where are you?', I asked in disbelief."

"I'm in a telephone box near the prison", he replied. "We have been released and we are walking to Ploiesti."

"When I put the phone down my mind was in turmoil. Gabriel, our eldest daughter, was able to take the car and go for her father, while I got in touch with the other wives. We had a memorable reunion and a great time of rejoicing, with thanksgivings to God for this deliverance. The end had come so suddenly and unexpectedly we just could not take it in."

The whole agonising process had lasted more than nine months. It had been difficult, but everyone agreed that it could have been much worse.

Mircea got his job back. For the remainder of the Communist period, life was reasonable; but there was always tension and fear.

To be a true believer and continue in church work took much courage. A mere professor would have been unable to survive. My final question to Mircea was "How did your faith stand up to the test?".

His response was, "The presence of God was a reality to me; I felt Him closer than at any other time in my life. I often cried when I was alone in my cell, but they were not tears of anger or frustration. It was a kind of inexplicable joy. I felt very much the prayers of my family and the church. In particular on Thursday nights, the night of our prayer meeting, I was even more conscious of the Lord with me."

"For part of our time in the prison we were together in a large room. A guard also lived with us. We all had memorised many Scriptures and we would quote these to each other to stimulate our minds and refresh our hearts. We would also quietly sing hymns. The guard never objected. He knew we were different from the other prisoners."

"Were there any special parts of Scripture that comforted you?" I asked.

"Yes!" he said, his face lighting up as he rubbed his hands with boyish excitement! "Yes! 1 John 2:6: *He that saith he abideth in him ought himself also to walk, even as he walked*".

After listening to this long story, we said Goodnight. As often happened in Romania, I lay alone with my thoughts. I had to admit that, despite any personal trials that had come my way, I had never really proved the meaning of the verse he quoted.

CHAPTER XVI

Dressed Up To Preach

L ife with the Romanian Christians was not all tension. I
recall one memorable outing, a welcome relaxation, at a
beautiful river valley near the foothills of the snow-topped
Fagaras Mountains.

Before settling for the afternoon we drove up to Bîlea Lake,
high up in the mountains. The road serpentined up the steep side
of forested, subtropical ravines and mountains, over bridges and
under snow guards. The praises of Nicolae Ceaucescu were
painted in banner headlines on the concrete parapets of all the
bridges!

It was a torturous climb for the overloaded Dacia cars, but we
made good progress. We were followed, at a discreet distance, by
the Securitate. There was one particular scenic spot where we
stopped and got out to admire the view and take some pictures. The
Police drove past us. We resumed our ascent, and about two miles
further up there was the police car with its engine cover open, and
steam bellowing out of the engine. It would climb no further that
day!

After our three car convoy passed, there were cries of elation and the clapping of hands. One of the younger passengers quipped, "God's cars are better than the Devil's!".

On our descent we stopped by a river for our picnic. We enjoyed playing, singing and feasting with these lovely families. The younger element cut down some branches of trees, broke them into sticks, and kindled a fire over which we barbecued some meat which had been made into hamburgers. The equipment was rudimentary, but effective. The food for this special treat, particularly the meat, had been purchased at considerable sacrifice.

The sky was dark blue, the sun intense, and birds flew overhead singing in joyous chorus. The river rattled over the stones and, as far as we knew, we were alone - a little band of people whose hearts God had touched. We sang to the accompaniment of a beautiful hand-made guitar -

When through the woods and forest glades I wander,
And hear the birds sing sweetly in the trees ...
Then sings my soul, my Saviour, God, to Thee,
How great Thou art!

Gerald and I sang in English, the rest in Romanian. Language was not a barrier in this act of worship.

A telling postscript to the picnic was that some of those who enjoyed the meal later had stomach disorders, due to not being used to eating so much rich food at one time!

At the conclusion of the outing we made what we thought was a social call, to Costica's parents' home in the village of Arpas. His mother, a most attractive and dominant lady, welcomed us into their home. His father had an infectious laugh and his eyes twinkled with mischievous delight. In the early part of the century, this very dear saint of God had been greatly used of the Lord to pioneer the gospel in this part of Transylvania.

We had not been there long when Gerald and I, at the command of Mrs. Morariu, were ushered into a bedroom. She thrust a set of folded clothes into each of our arms and gestured that we put them on. She then left us.

Mesmerised, we unfolded the clothes and stared at what we had been given. It was a full rig-out of Romanian National dress: white trousers, white embroidered overshirt, a large belt and black waistcoat!

"I couldn't wear these!", I exclaimed to Gerald.

"Brother, we have little option", he replied, with a nervous laugh.

So we set about transforming ourselves from casual Westerners to formal Romanians! When we emerged in our costumes, which fitted perfectly, there were whoops of delight. We both felt very embarrassed, and didn't know how to respond properly to this seemingly very high honour.

Morariu Senior then said through an interpreter, "It's time now to go to the church. They will be waiting for us."

Gerald said, with alarm in his voice, "We have been out for some recreation; no one said we were going to a meeting! We are not prepared, we do not have our Bibles."

My main concern was for myself: what on earth did I look like? "We can't go like THIS!", I added with some emphasis.

Our protests were in vain. Very quickly they produced two English Bibles. We were marched down the street in procession, with the villagers looking on! Although we felt decidedly uncomfortable at the experience, it was evident that we were bringing joy to these dear folk.

The place where they convened their meetings was no more than a glorified outhouse, a lean-to against another building. We entered, and as we did so a murmuring of delight went through the congregation. The place was full of people, and nearly all of them, men and women, were dressed in ceremonial costumes!

It had all been so well planned, and for our benefit!

Once again the Iach family were present, and sang to the accompaniment of their various instruments. Then we preached. Preaching in Romanian costume was a delight! The wide sleeves of the shirt allowed the maximum amount of ventilation on that very humid evening! The text I chose was Romans 1:16, *"For I am not ashamed of the gospel of Christ: for it is the power of God unto salvation to every one that believes"*.

As before, *"salvation came to the house"*. There were tears of repentance and rejoicing. The Word of the Lord found an abiding place in hungry hearts.

After the meeting we returned to the Morariu home for a supper in the open air, under the vines. It was a brilliant, starlit night. Over twenty people were present on that happy occasion. I helped myself to generous portions of maize bread and buffalo milk. I had become very fond of the latter!

All too quickly, the time came to divest ourselves of the comfortable Romanian costumes. I must confess to a secret attachment to them! When we had changed back into our own clothes we had a time of prayer together. We said our farewells and the mandatory 'Maranathas'. Another memorable day was drawing to a close.

And all the while, at the edge of the village, the Secret Police patiently waited for our departure.

CHAPTER XVII

The Youthful Translator

At this time, before one meeting in Sibiu, Gerald and I were introduced to a dark-haired, very young girl - or so she seemed to us. She was nineteen years old. One of the elders said "This is your translator for the meeting"!

"What is your name?" I asked, wondering how such a young person would cope with translating two messages.

"I am Doina", she replied confidently, in perfect English. There was something about her response that immediately reassured us that all would be well. And it was!

This simple introduction was our first communication in the Spirit. Not only did this young woman have an excellent command of good English, but in her heart there was a passionate love for the Saviour. For us, and many other visiting speakers, there was complete trust, not only in her linguistic ability, but in her uncanny sense of interpreting the preachers' thoughts.

Each time we returned to the Sibiu area she would devote herself to being our constant companion, and we could discuss at length the hazards and shortcomings of translation. Preaching through an interpreter is completely different from speaking directly to people in one's native language. Down the years I had often listened to missionaries giving anecdotes on this topic, amusing and otherwise, as they rehearsed the mistakes and misunderstandings. Now I was at the sharp end, how was I coping? "Not very well", came the instant and curt response from Doina on one occasion. "All your headings began with the letter 'C', in English!"

"What's wrong with that?", I quizzed. She laughed, and said "When I put them into Romanian they all begin with different letters!". My attention to emphasis and memory-retaining techniques had been useless!

On another occasion I quoted (or tried to quote) some verses from a well known hymn. We struggled through this, and I saw that she was in some discomfort. When the meeting was over I said, "Did I give you a problem tonight?" "Yes", she said. "What you quoted didn't rhyme in Romanian, and I had to wait until you had said enough to give the sense of the content!" This was another gentle, but necessary, rebuke.

A rather amusing incident took place during one of the early visits to Sibiu. Because there was no one who could translate direct from English to Romanian, it was necessary to translate first from English into German and then from German into Romanian! The original message in English was understood by very few, so there was little or no reaction. The German translation was understood by some, and I could see a glimmer of interest in their faces. When the German was translated into Romanian there was total concentration: smiles appeared and heads nodded! It was hard to keep the next sentence in mind, while the previous one was being translated; but after a few hesitations I got into a routine. Occasionally I forgot the second translator, and was continuing before he had time to do his translation. At one point, when I had done this, he ejaculated something in Romanian, and there was quite a volume of laughter. Later I found out that he had shouted, "My turn!".

On one visit a friend from Belfast was with me, and he was giving his testimony in the large church in Bucharest. His first words were "Earlier in the meeting I was impressed by the words a brother read in the Gospel of John, chapter 20: *"Whom seekest thou?"*. The translator said, "Pardon?" - So he repeated the phrase. The translator looked puzzled! "I don't understand", he said, "which verse is it?". At that point I whispered to my friend, "Say: *"Who are you looking for?"*. He did, and all was well!

As time passed, one of the more serious aspects of translation surfaced, when I learned that, in some passages, the accepted Romanian version of the Scriptures was significantly different to the Authorised text, which I was using. I resorted to asking the translator to read back to me, in English, what the Romanian version was saying. In most cases it was almost the same, and in some instances it gave a better translation. But in some important points of doctrine the real meaning was unclear, or even inaccurate.

This led to debates, and sometimes intense arguments. Even at home, in conversational Bible studies, different views, interpretations and applications can lead to endless and often fruitless discussion; so it is not difficult to see the complications that can arise when the problem is compounded by a different language, and with people who have different thought patterns.

Perhaps for the first time in my Christian experience, I became very sensitive to my absolute reliance on the Holy Spirit. Each message, each preaching, was based on the belief that the Spirit would interpret the Word to the hearers.

There had also to be implicit trust in the translator. But there were times when there was no opportunity to discuss a message beforehand, and we would be introduced just as the meeting commenced. On such occasions I would urgently cry to the Lord; but sometimes the translator would not grasp the message and say, "Please repeat", or "What did you say?", or "Sorry, I don't understand!" or even on one or two occasions, "I don't agree with you!". Perspiration flowed freely, the heart thumped so that I could hear it, and the saliva dried up in my mouth. In these circumstances, it was best to curtail the message, or if possible change it mid-stream! The learning curve was steep. Yet, over and over again, the Spirit of the Lord came in power.

I often discussed the problems with Doina and other reliable translators. Should they deliver a direct transfer of words and sentences, or should they have the liberty to use their own words, more akin to their way of understanding, to give the true sense of the message?

We came to the conclusion that, where the speaker and the translator are not familiar with each other, it would be necessary to ask for word for word transfer, or as near as possible. But we also agreed that a good translator who was in touch with the Lord, and who was familiar with the speaker's diction and his thought and word processes, should have the liberty to rephrase or replace words to suit the local vernacular and context. We felt that this could be done to good effect without the translator becoming the preacher or re-interpreting the message.

At one meeting I watched and listened intently as a Romanian translated for a visiting American speaker. It was evident that there was a very good understanding between them. The translator seemed at ease, and I thought 'he's a good translator'. At the end of the meeting, on the way home, I told my translator what I thought. He looked at me, smiled, and said "He (the other translator) preaches a good message!".

The blessings from the spoken word, however, have far out-weighed any difficulties that have arisen because of problems with translation. The God whom we proclaim is Sovereign, and His promise is true: *"My word ... shall not return to me void, but it shall accomplish that which I please, and it shall prosper in the thing whereto I sent it"* (Isa 55:11).

CHAPTER XVIII

Re-Crossing The Frontier

Prior to the Revolution all my travels to and from Romania were over land. My return journey with Gerald in 1987, through the Romanian-Hungarian frontier at Nadalac, remains vivid in my memory.

Apart from some Romanian mementoes given to us by friends, we had little of importance in the car. Or so I thought!

I did have some recordings of choir and community singing, and interviews with elders on tape. I also had five exposed films. I had taken with me twenty Kodak slide films for the use of one or two Romanian Christians whom I knew to have an interest in photography. However, they had no facilities to process them; so I removed them from their cardboard containers and put them in a plastic bag with the five exposed films, to bring home.

At the border the Customs officer, closely shadowed by a plain clothes official (whom I took to be Securitate) took my recordings and films. He also searched my clothing and took my diary and wallet. In my diary I had many addresses of contacts, which friends had insisted on giving me, despite my protests on security grounds.

"We are not worried", they said. "We trust the Lord in this, so you must not worry either. Please do not forget us. Write to us." I couldn't disappoint them, so I allowed them to write their own addresses in the diary. Then I would be sure that I had the correct spelling!

Now my worst fears were being realised.

What would the authorities do with the material they had confiscated? Would I get it all back? Or, more importantly, would my friends be endangered? I could not help chastising myself that I had given in to taking the addresses. I was also sensitive to the fact that I was a comparative newcomer to cross-frontier conditions, and I wondered if it would be a black mark against my name, or Gerald's.

While these thoughts were running around in my mind, I saw the Customs official leave the plastic bag on a window ledge of the building and go inside without it, thus enabling me to keep my eye on it. I then realised that another officer was making a meticulous search of the car. Everything moveable was taken out. He made a careful examination of the roof cloth, door panels, hubcaps ... Nothing escaped his attention. Gerald was sitting on the bonnet of the car, eating an orange. How could he be so relaxed! He jumped off to allow the officer to examine the engine and, when that was completed, he resumed his seat. We did not speak to each other.

The officer who had taken my bag eventually returned, carrying it with him. He gave me back my personal effects, the tapes, my wallet and diary. He then opened the plastic bag with the films and said, "you have many films!".

"Most of them are unused", I replied. "We are tourists, and take a lot of pictures." He reached into the bag, took one film out, and opened it up. It was a new one! He screwed on the lid, and did the same with two more. Both of these were new as well! He handed them back, gave us our passports and told us to proceed! As the soldier lifted the barrier, he looked around furtively, "Do you have any cigarettes?", he asked. Gratefully, he accepted a packet of polo mints!

Once into Hungary we stopped the car, looked at each other, and thanked the Lord for all that had transpired on our visit. We commended the special friends whom we had left behind to Him, and very especially those who might soon be in difficulties because of the information on tape and in the diary. We then continued on our journey. It was not until we were travelling through Germany that Gerald got out of the car, opened the bonnet and took from somewhere a flat plastic bag.

It contained a document detailing the persecutions of some prominent Christians and the disappearance of a University lec-turer who had publicly confessed his faith in Christ. The donor of the documents had requested that it be passed on to Radio Free Europe. The idea was that it should be broadcast back into Eastern Europe in an attempt to embarrass the Romanian authorities, who proclaimed that there was religious freedom in their country!

Such revelations would endanger the "Most Favoured Nation Status"privilege, and information like this would expose the situation as it really was. I subsequently learned that the message was broadcast back into Romania.

On our next visit I made a point of speaking to as many of the addressees in my diary, as possible. I was greatly relieved to find that there had been no inquisitions by the State. For this time, at least, the Lord had protected them from harrassment.

CHAPTER XIX

One Of Romania's Storehouses

D uring our 1989 visit we had the privilege of travelling
north to Moldavia. My companions on this trip were two
friends from Scotland who had offered me a seat in their
car. Moldavia lies in the extreme north-east of Romania and has
boundaries with the Ukraine in the north, and the former USSR
republic, Moldova, in the east.

The politics of the region are far from happy. Moldova was part
of Romania until the end of the Second World War, when it was
annexed and taken over by the Soviets to form one of the smallest
of the sixteen republics making up the USSR. That portion known
as Moldavia, which remains a part of Romania, is a province of
excellent horses and rich folklore. Some of Romania's best
vineyards lie between the two principal cities of Iasi and Suceava
(pronounced Yashy and Sushava).

When the principalities of Moldavia and Wallachia united in
1859 (an important date in the Northern Ireland spiritual calen-
dar!), Iasi served as the national capital, until replaced by Bucharest in 1862. This illustrious history accounts for the great

monasteries, churches, public buildings and museums, which are a constant surprise to visitors who had previously never heard of the place! Romania's first university was founded here in 1860. Although this area gets many visitors, the rest of Moldavia is well off the beaten track.

The purpose of our visit was to purchase, in the principal hotel in Suceava, food for the Christians meeting in the Brethren church, and their associates. Our guides and fellow travellers for the three day trip were two friends from Brasov. They travelled with us in my friend's Austin Montega car. From the outset they, more than we perhaps, fully appreciated the risk they were taking in travelling in a Western car and associating with foreign travellers, as this was forbidden by law.

We had travelled about forty miles when, in heavy rain, we were flagged down by a uniformed Militia man. Not wishing to expose our Romanian friends, our driver got out of the car to talk with the police. He was told we had broken the speed limit!

He was in no position to dispute this. We had been having a lively debate about the Christian's salvation being eternally secure in Christ, and our minds were not on the speed! Without any argument, and to get away from the Militia as quickly and quietly as possible, he paid the on-the-spot fine and we resumed our journey. There were hefty sighs of relief all round!

Half an hour later we were flagged down again, and there was a repeat performance. We had allegedly broken the speed limit; only this time we were certain that we were under the limit. However he made no protest, as it was too dangerous. The second fine was paid and we were again on our way, angry at the injustice of it. But our Romanian friends contented themselves by saying, "What can you expect? This is Romania!".

We had a picnic of cheese sandwiches and juice in the car, and arrived in Suceava in the early afternoon. When we reached the hotel where we were to purchase the food, we were discreetly greeted by a number of men. It turned out that they were the leaders of the local church, who had come to help us load and transport the food.

As in all transactions, the goods could be purchased only with Western currency. Since it was illegal for Romanians to have any, our friends had to make out a list of their requirements so that we could buy on their behalf. We told them how many dollars we had for this purpose, and calculations were made as to how much of each item we could afford.

It was quite surprising to find that, for the next two hours, these eight men allowed themselves to be seen carrying food from the basement of this Spartan and unattractive building to the waiting vehicles - two very run-down cars, and a cross between a car and a van. They loaded the vehicles and made a number of journeys to the Prayer House (the local Brethren church), about two miles away, on the outskirts of the city.

The basement store of the hotel was a veritable Aladdin's Cave. It was amply stocked with all kinds of basic bagged and tinned food. There was also an abundance of hardware: fridges, freezers, cookers, televisions, radios, cycles, vehicle tyres, engine oil. You name it, it was there!

At times like this my heart was heavy. To think that the thousands of inhabitants of this city, and all other cities and towns in Romania, would stand in line for hours at appointed places for basic food, while there was food in abundance in their very midst!

It was clear to me that not all Romanians were in want. The privileged few with special associations and influence lived like kings. It was enough to try the patience of a saint!

For this assignment, our main purchases were flour, sugar and coffee. It was hard work, as it was packed in bulk and therefore heavy and awkward. It had to be man-handled up a flight of rough concrete steps on to the street, and then loaded on to the vehicles. There were many willing hands at the church, mainly women and children. An outside building, separated from the church building, had been emptied and cleaned up. We filled it from floor to ceiling.

I knew from previous experience that the bulk of the coffee would be for re-sale. It was a precious commodity, and produced very valuable revenue, which would then be distributed among the very many large families. It was common to find ten or twelve children in each family. We noted also, especially in the villages in this northern part of Moldavia, that most of the children and some of the adults were in their bare feet.

When all the necessary items had been paid for, transported and stored, a very happy band of people knelt in the church to return thanks to their Lord. In quick succession, and with tears of joy, they thanked Him for His faithfulness to them, and for the friends who had come so far to bring them material help and spiritual encouragement.

Last minute border checks.

"Steady as you go!"

Fritz Weber with Author outside the Sibiu Prayer House.
September 1993.

Costica and Fritz with the material for the Sibiu Church building.

Outside Sibiu Church after service.
(Foreground, Dacia car with Securitate number plate).

Dressed up to preach.

Distributing literature

First evangelistic meeting in village hall.

Costica preaching prior to a baptism.
(Candidates in the foreground)

Badulesti - early days March 1990. (Fritz translating for Gerald).
(Before new Prayer House was built).

New Prayer House in Sibiu.

New Prayer House in Badulesti.

Doina.

Gerald.

Nina and Eldad Teodosiu (1984).

Zoar Orphanage, Talmacui. Some of the children.

The former Securitate Observation Tower and one of the orphan houses at Uracani.

CHAPTER XX

Romania's Library Lady

Jeni Rosian is one of the most remarkable young women I have
met in Romania. She was born in Moldavia in Northern
Romania. Her parents were poor. Life was hard. Speaking
with affection about her mother, she poured out her heart to me
about those early days.

"My mother received a job in a factory four miles from our
town. She had to travel every day by train, in old wagons without
light or heat. The windows were broken, and the doors wouldn't
close properly. In the winter the wind was so strong and the cold
so intense, that many times when she arrived home at twelve
o'clock at night she was weak and exhausted."

"My mother was a hero", she continued. "Through her prayers
and devotion to God, He kept her and our family safe."

"We had family prayers every day. First we sang some songs,
then my mother would read something, and we knelt to pray.
Mother prayed first - sometimes for twenty minutes! She opened

her heart to the Lord, with her many problems which, as children, we did not understand. My father prayed next. His prayers were shorter! Then we children prayed, one by one."

"In school we were indoctrinated into the Pioneer (Young Communist) Organisation. This provoked strong competition amongst the pupils. I became boss of the class." She laughed at the memory. It was obvious that, in those early days, she had developed a strong personality which would stand her in good stead in days to come.

Then, in her early teens, she accepted the Saviour, believing that He had died for her sins at Calvary. It was a simple, uncomplicated faith. Her life subsequently proved the reality of her new birth.

Through her intelligence and hard work, she won a place at the university in Ploiesti, two hundred and fifty miles south of her home. She graduated in 1983 as a Mechanical Engineer. While at university she met with the Christians in the Brethren church in Ploiesti, where she had a special interest in the work amongst children. Her artistic flair and innovative creations amused and captivated the "copii" (Romanian for children).

When it was time to look for a job in the Petro Chemical Industry, she was given a choice, and chose to travel north to Medias, where she knew there was a large, active church. She joined the Gas Company and worked there until after the Revolution; but all the time working with the local children. The Factory Director allotted her a room of her own in a block of flats.

"It was Grade Five", she said. "I couldn't believe that they would give me this grade. It was the lowest! Grade 1 accommodation was large; Grade 2, smaller; Grade 3, smaller still; Grade 4, just one small room with a bathroom; Grade 5, a tiny room, with a bathroom shared by everyone on the same floor."

"It was very damp, so I wrote to the newspaper and told them about this terrible place, where the rubbish was taken away by the wind and the rain, people fought in the corridors with knives, and prostitutes caused problems."

"I soon got another little flat to rent, and began to teach the children in the block about Jesus. For the next four years, each evening I travelled to villages by bus and train to teach children. It was dangerous, and the Authorities wanted to move me."

"What have I done wrong?" I asked them. "The Securitate had complained to the Factory Director, asking him to write a bad report about me."

"But he replied, 'She's making her job well. I do not make any report on her free time!' "

"So they left me alone. God protected me. Eventually I decided to buy a little flat. The flat was costing 80,000 lei, and I had 5,000 lei! When I spoke to the Factory Director, and he asked me how much money I had, he said 'You are crazy!'."

"The same day I received a letter from a Christian in Germany, who did not write to me very often. He quoted one verse of Scripture: *"My God shall supply all your need according to his riches in glory by Christ Jesus"* (Philippians 4:19). I took this as an answer! A friend put up the money for my flat and I worked until I had paid it off. I sewed clothes, painted, made things, sleeping only two or three hours every night!"

"The next stage in my work for the Lord was translating for Child Evangelism Fellowship. I secretly received many CEF aids for my work with the children. The Orthodox priests began to write many lies about me in the papers but, Praise God, I was left alone to continue with my precious work for Him."

When the Revolution came Jeni was liberated to serve the Lord in a way she had not expected.

Gusty, her husband, took up the story. "Jeni had an idea to start a Christian lending library, so I said 'OK - start! But how?'. Within a few days she came home very excited. 'I have seen a house for sale, and I want to buy it for a library' she told me!"

"How much?", I asked her.

" '270,000 lei', she replied, "her voice not even wavering!"

Gusty told me "Her salary was 2,000 lei per month." He looked at Jeni and smiled, then he continued, "But she is a very determined lady!".

"She borrowed 100,000 lei and agreed to pay 170,000 lei in dollars, believing that *"the Lord would supply all her need"*. She was so sure, and I couldn't stop her! All this happened just before we were married."

"Our wedding day was 24th March 1990. During the wedding, a lorry arrived from Holland and a brother told us that he had a printing press for us! This was a very big surprise for both of us, but a pleasant interruption to our celebrations. Then, when we had almost finished our wedding feast, two ladies arrived from England! I said to Jeni, 'This is too much. We need to be alone!'"

"The ladies said that they were delivering some pieces of equipment, but they could not stay. One of them took some dollars from her bag. 'This is for you', she said, and pushed the money into Jeni's hand. 'It is from a group of Christians in England. We have been all round Romania and could not find any place to leave this. Then we were told about you. This is for your new library!'"

"When they left", Gusti continued, "we counted the money. It was $2,000 - enough to pay off the 170,000 lei in dollars, with some left over!"

"Praise God! He had proved himself real. He was with us and knew our hearts. He **did** supply our need."

Jeni continued. "On 15th May 1990 we opened the library - after work, work, work! Visitors began to bring us books, from all kinds of places. In Ceaucescu's time, many Christians in Romania had books hidden away. Sometimes there would be three or four of the same title, so this built up our stock. People began to queue up to borrow from the library."

"When 'Open Doors' printed a picture of our library in their magazine, we discovered we had a prayer partner. Many months before all these happenings, a lady in England was praying. As she prayed, she very distinctly heard the name 'Jenny'. So she began to pray for 'Jenny'. In her church there was a lady, also called Jenny and she wondered why she was being prompted to pray for her! When she enquired gently if she had a problem, she said 'It's not me! but you continue to pray for Jenny. God will tell you who she is.'"

"So when she read about me in the Open Doors' magazine, she discovered who she had been praying for. She wrote to me, and I realised that her special prayer support had given me the faith to continue."

"Before my father died in 1993 he told me that, during the important time of setting up the library, he had fasted and prayed for me for eighteen days! How I miss his prayers; I feel so unworthy at the sacrifice he made for me, but it was for God's work."

The library is now functioning in Medias, and many books are borrowed, read and returned. The printing press is in operation, under Gusti's control; and many booklets and tracts, both for adults and children, are published regularly and distributed throughout Romania. In 1994 it was a real thrill for me to receive a Romanian copy of "How to Teach the Tabernacle" by Dr. David Gooding.

"During this year", Jeni continued, "God has blessed the library work in a special way." Their dreams for more space came true, they now have four new rooms upstairs and have been able to install central heating.

She explained, "We have started a new activity: a Sunday School teachers' library by post! These materials are very expensive, and we hope that the people who borrow them will return them in good condition."

"For Christmas we printed five thousand copies of the tract 'The Mystery of Christmas'. Immediately after this we received from England five thousand copies of 'Jesus, the Man who Changed History'."

"The best news is that we have signed a contract in England for the fitting out of a printing office. We must pay 50,000 DM over the next five years. If we work hard we can manage it. God has shown us His love through all these things, and we are so thankful to Him."

As I listened to the unfolding of this amazing story I felt ashamed. In my heart I heard again the Master's words *"Oh ye of little faith"*. I have no doubt that in a coming day many will rise to bless the name of this simple, courageous lady and her faithful husband.

CHAPTER XXI

A New Prayer House In Sibiu

I n 1984 great pressure was being put on the leaders of the Sibiu Romanian 'Brethren Church'. (In Romanian, this translates to 'Christians according to the Gospel'.)

The upstairs room in which they met, where I had the experience with the weeping translator, was part of a large State owned factory. The Management wanted to repossess it. As time passed, more and more pressure was exerted by the authorities, and the leaders of the church were becoming more desperate. Regular prayer meetings were held, and days of fasting appointed. When we left after that first visit, no alternative accommodation had been found. The elders wanted to find a site and build. However, in conditions of hostility to anything religious, this seemed only a remote possibility.

When we returned in 1987, three years later, no suitable premises had been found, and the situation was very tense. The authorities were threatening eviction, with promises of helping them to find another place. They wanted a quick resolution to the problem.

It was a stick and carrot situation!

Over the years the members of the congregation had been giving sacrificially, for the provision of a new building. Some were even contributing one week's wage per month. Grace was out-stepping law! The tithe, required under the Mosaic law, was being more than doubled by dedicated Christians who loved their Lord.

The cumulative total of such offerings in monetary terms would not have seemed high by Western standards; but it was a sacrifice of a sweet savour to the Lord. I had to confess that I had never, on a regular basis, given a week's salary per month to the Lord. The Building Society got it!

I was beginning to see that love for the Lord and His testimony went right to the heart of the matter. Like the Thessalonian believers, the Romanians were *"giving of their own selves to the Lord"* (2 Cor. 8:5). They had no other priorities, and I was overwhelmed at the extraordinary faith in God and their courage in standing up to State pressure and persecution.

At this time the Securitate created situations, in an endeavour to trap the Christians into breaking the law, so that they could be arrested and punished.

One of my friends said to me, "They tried to kill me three times. A bus was almost rammed into my car at traffic lights. I thought 'stupid driver!', and forgot about the incident. On the same day the following week, Thursday, while I was on my way to church I saw the same bus, in the same area. Just as I was wondering where I had seen it before, I suddenly realised that it was being driven at me! It was a miracle that I was able to avoid him. I realised that these two incidents were connected, and that the Securitate were out either to kill or injure me, or at least to get me involved in an accident. I was absolutely persuaded of this when, the following week, for the third time, the same bus almost ran me down! Praise God, I escaped."

It was not unusual for church elders to be taken from their work places to the Securitate office, detained overnight, and returned to work the next morning. This could be repeated for up to three or four days. Sometimes physical beatings took place, but in most cases it was verbal threats, a kind of psychological torture. This was very severe on families who usually had no idea where their loved ones were. Even if they suspected what was happening, there was nothing they could do but tell the Lord and the church. It was all being recorded in heaven.

We were privileged to see just a tiny part of the great mosaic of their lives. We asked no questions - talk was costly. Behind the smiles, warm embraces and moving worship, we could sense the tension.

Many Christians, mainly from Northern Ireland, gave generously to the fund for the new church building in Sibiu. Their contributions amounted to approximately 80% of the total cost. The Lord honoured the believers' faith, and a site was granted and procured, a stone's throw from their old meeting place!

My friend continued, "Prior to this, the owners of the factory which we occupied offered us a large shed-type building that was part of a mental institution. It was used to keep animals for meat for the hospital. They said 'you can go there along with the mad people'. We immediately said No!"

"Shortly after this the Factory manager called us to his office and told us to 'get out', and it was 'the final warning'. We urged him to come to our meeting place at the end of our regular Thursday evening prayer and teaching meeting, to talk with our elders. Much to our surprise, he agreed to come!"

"When he entered the building, we called him to the front and introduced him to the congregation. We all stood up and some brothers began to pray, thanking God that the Director had come to see and hear their cries for a new building. They prayed that God would bless him and his family. He became troubled in his heart when he heard these prayers, and his attitude changed. We knew then that he really wanted to help us."

"He said to us 'What place can I give you in exchange?'. A brother from the back of the church stood up and said 'I know you have a place on Vopsitorilor Street - the old store. It would be good for a new building. Can you give that to us?'"

"The Director said 'If you want this, I will give it to you with all my heart!'. So the whole church went to the place and the unanimous decision was 'Yes, we like it; we will take it!'."

Fritz and Costica then entered into negotiations with the Director. As it happened, he was a close colleague of Nici Ceaucescu, the President's son, who was the Governor of Sibiu County. He told them to prepare a letter of request to him, to get his father's approval for the building.

"Each morning when the President's son drove to work, he would run from the car with his guards to his office, and people would push letters into his hand. Fritz and I decided that we would use this tactic to get our letter of request to him. So one morning we stood waiting for him, and managed to hand over the letter. It so happened that there weren't too many other people about. He signed it, and it was eventually delivered to the President's Secretary in Bucharest - with whom he was very 'friendly'. He told her to get his father's signature some day when he was busy, by slipping it in among other normal papers. She did this and, when the President saw his son's signature already on the letter, he also signed it, without reading it! So this signature secured for the church in Sibiu the approval for the site and the building of their new Prayer House!"

During all this time, a period of some months, the church fasted and prayed every Monday and Thursday.

"The next step", Costica continued, "was to draw up a contract with the Factory Director, for the exchange of buildings. Part of the agreement was that the factories throughout Romania would help in getting building materials, for which we would pay, and the factory also promised to help with technical assistance. So the agreement was signed. In our circumstances, this was most unusual."

Before the building work commenced, Fritz took us to see the location. I was very apprehensive at what I saw. The approach was through a very narrow street in the oldest part of the city. The old store had to be demolished; and I thought it seemed a most unattractive proposition. But these were men of vision, they could see what I couldn't. They assured me that this was the correct location. They would build there to the glory of God, and it would be completed in a little over one year. I was taken aback at their confidence and faith.

It was rare for the Authorities to grant approval for the erection of a building for Christian worship. But the trauma over the previous three years and the anxiety of the Authorities to have them moved, contributed greatly to the issuing of approval, and, not least, the signature of the Romanian President! Above all this of course, and at a different level, the Unseen and Eternal were at work to accomplish the Divine purpose. It was another example of God using *"the wrath of man to praise him"*.

The work commenced in 1988. A friend who lived round the corner from the site gave up part of his accommodation, for a small fee, as a dining room for the workers. One or two of the women from the church faithfully prepared meals for all who needed them, including the visitors. We ate there on at least two occasions. There was soup - plenty of it - bread, chicken, pork, coffee, tea, cake! The menu varied, but there was always an adequate supply.

These were very happy times. There was a lot of good humour, and the locals were just thrilled to share with us. They proudly conducted us through the forest of wooden scaffolding, up and down the not-too-safe ladders, in and out through mortar, cement, timber, and everything that constitutes a building site working at full throttle.

It was at this time that I learned how they had managed to operate so well under their Communist masters. When they came to build the church the Director said that he did not have anybody who could give them technical assistance. So Fritz and Costica took unpaid leave from work, and supervised the construction. At the end of three months, they both agreed that they could not continue. It was becoming impossible to feed their families. They had had to be content with eating bread and pork fat!

They both prayed, and one day Costica said to Fritz, "We cannot live any more this way, so we will have to ask the Director for technical assistance. If he says No, then we will offer to be the technical assistants, in accordance with the contract, paid by him, if he will arrange for us to be released from our own factories."

They followed the idea through, and the Director agreed within a day! They were immediately released from their normal jobs and their pay transferred to the Factory Director who was happy to let them continue to supervise the building of the church. They were able to return to their own jobs when the building was complete.

After listening to the story, I said to Costica, "This is like a fairy tale!". He smiled and said, "Dumnezeu (God) did it!"

All the Christians in the church said "This has never happened before: Communists paying Christians to build their church!".

With the special authorisation paper from the contract, the two Communist-paid Supervisors travelled the length and breadth of

Romania to other factories, to collect building materials. They also managed to get a Securitate vehicle registration number for the car they used! Normally another vehicle accompanied this car, and neither vehicle was ever stopped or searched!

I drove in this blue Dacia many times, but never knew the significance of the registration number!

As well as building materials, these vehicles were used to carry the many Bibles taken from boats on the Danube and from other secret locations in Northern Romania. Their dedicated drivers delivered them, at great personal risk, to individual homes, church buildings, and other safe places.

I asked Costica, "How did you know when to go for the Bibles?". He confirmed what Mircea had told me about using the book of Proverbs as the code.

Referring back to the vehicles they used for transportation, Costica told me that one of the church members worked in a factory which made strong springs. He made some which they fitted to the 'special' cars, so that when they were loaded they just looked normal!

Through friends they arranged for the heating equipment for the church building to be supplied from Germany. When it was time to bring it to Sibiu, Fritz, Costica and his son, Costel, went to the border to collect it. The Securitate were waiting for them! They were questioned for five hours, after which they were told that the driver of the van had been instructed to take the equipment back to Germany.

This was a bitter disappointment. It was then one o'clock in the morning, so they had no option but to stay in a hotel in Arad, and return to Sibiu in the morning. The police followed them on their journey.

A special meeting of the church was called, and Fritz reported "They are not allowing us to have the heating. But we have a great God, who can still do it for us!" They agreed to fast on Mondays and Thursdays. "We cried together", confessed Costica.

He continued, "After three weeks the bosses at the factory called us, and said 'Your heating system has arrived along with some parts for our factory. You can come and collect it!' We were stunned for a moment, but we quickly realised that God had answered our prayers. The brothers in the church said, 'How does it happen that in a country as big as Germany, the communists take the trouble to bring the heating for a Christian church in Romania at their expense?'"

They completed the building, which accommodates six hundred people, and opened it just after the Revolution. It was a tribute to God's faithfulness to His children. As expected, that first meeting was full to overflowing, with many standing outside.

Christians attended from other countries, and the local Romanians flocked to this unique event. Alternating tears and smiles were the order of the day! For Costica and Fritz there was a great sense of relief, and it was difficult for them to hide their pride in the new building. They paid unreserved tribute to the brothers and sisters of the Sibiu church who had worked tirelessly, and contributed sacrificially.

JESUS CHRIST IS LORD, the often displayed text in church buildings in the West, was now the dominant feature in this new building. Kingdoms rise and fall, rulers come and go, but He, our Lord Jesus Christ, remains LORD.

What a testimony in the face of forty-five years of Marxist ideology!

CHAPTER XXII

Freedom - "God Is With Us"

Whi le things appeared as normal within Romanian soc- iety, and the completion of the Sibiu church approached, momentous events were taking place in Eastern Eu- rope. Country after country in the Eastern bloc was convulsed in revolution. Totalitarian regimes collapsed under the sheer weight of People Power. The sight of great chunks of concrete being gouged out of the Berlin Wall made compulsive television view- ing.

"When do you think freedom will come to Romania?", I was asked repeatedly. The corollary to this was, "How long do you think it will take?". Those who had personal experience of Romania could not really conceive of any circumstance that would bring about such a situation.

It was said that one in four of Romania's population was an informer, or involved in some collaboration with the State authori- ties. The Securitate would know of the slightest murmur of discontent, and it would be dealt with instantly.

Fear ruled!

There was unrelenting violence. It was impossible to see how the iron grip could be broken; but suddenly, unexpectedly, it was.

The overthrow of President Nicolae Ceaucescu and his infamous wife, Elena, came like an electric shock to the Western world. On Christmas Day 1989, there was no "peace on earth" in Romania, and certainly no "goodwill to men". The Romanian struggle had begun!

I telephoned my friend Gerhardt in Brazov. It had seemed pointless to do this, so I was very surprised when, within one minute, I was connected and Gerhardt answered.

"Where are you?", he responded to my greeting.

"In Ireland", I replied. "How are you?"

"Listen!", said Gerhardt, and I could distinctly hear the crack of gunfire.

The battle for the control of Brasov was at its peak!

"Thank God, we are all well and, so far, safe", he continued.

"Do you have any news about other Christians?", I enquired. "Have there been any casualties?"

"No, we don't know of any; the Christians are staying off the streets!" I assured him of our love and prayers, and asked him to convey this to the rest of my friends, as opportunity allowed.

It was a short, but dramatic conversation. Immediately my tension was released, but as we carried on with our Christmas celebration my heart was really with those in turmoil, so far away. Within ten days this beautiful, caged country had taken the first tentative steps towards throwing off the iron yoke of Communism.

"Freedom!" "Democracy!" "God is with us!", were the cries of the crowds.

All the visible trappings of Ceaucescu - the signposts, banners and posters - were ripped from their places of prominence. Things would never be the same again. Crowds thronged the streets. Car horns continuously hooted their cacophony of triumph. Factories, offices, transport, were all at a standstill. The communist insignia was cut out of the Romanian National flag. Everywhere there was the incongruous sight of the red, yellow and blue tricolour with the hole in the centre. No longer was it the Socialist Republic of Romania: it was now just Romania!

Through the mail on 2nd January 1990 I received the first positive evidence that the frontier was opened. The letter was from Jeni in Medias. The postmark was dated 21st December 1989. Boldly printed on the envelope, beside my address, were the words FREEDOM - "GOD IS WITH US".

I reckon this envelope must be pretty near a collector's item!

Some of the Christians were challenged as to why they had not come down on to the streets to fight for freedom.

"Why did you leave it to others?", they were asked.

The response was sound and sincere: "We did not seek revolution, or want a battle for freedom. We accepted the rule of our country, though it was very hard. We prayed that we would be faithful witnesses in the darkest days. We did not agitate for change. Our Lord knew our circumstances. When the fighting came, we continued to pray for the salvation of our country. We knew that the Lord would accomplish His own purposes."

In June 1989 I had retired from my employment with the Northern Ireland Civil Service, and July found me once again in Romania! Now the door through which I had been coming and going for five years was taken right off its hinges!

In March 1990, I travelled to Stuttgart by air and rendezvoused with my Scottish friends in Metzingen, where there is a large ex-patriot Romanian Brethren church. We purchased a second hand VW Golf car for one of the Romanian workers and filled it with basic foodstuffs. After an overnight stop, a small group met early on a crisp morning to pray and commend us to the Lord. At 6.00 a.m., accompanied by one of the local young men in a van loaded with food and clothing, we left, and drove, without sleep, to the Romanian border.

What would it be like? The uncertainty of what lay ahead made it seem as though we were entering a new country!

At four o'clock next morning we parked the car two miles before the border, and tried to sleep. It was difficult, even though we were all very weary. The high expectation of what a free Romania would be like successfully worked against us, so at six o'clock we decided to proceed! All the tension and fear which I had experienced in previous crossings was absent. Nevertheless, we did cast ourselves upon the Lord, and asked for a safe passage and an equally safe journey to our destination.

CHAPTER XXIII

A New Beginning

T he Customs post at Arad was chaotic! Vehicles of every size and description were being waved through by jubilant Customs Officials.

"We're importing this vehicle", I said directly to the uniformed Customs man. He showed us where to go, so we joined a small queue, handed in the vehicle details to be stamped, and in twenty minutes we were on our way! They had not asked to see our passports, nor checked the contents of the car or van. There was an atmosphere of gay abandon!

All the old landmarks were the same. We drove through the familiar lane where on previous occasions we had waited tensely for hours. The crude hut where I was strip-searched was empty and forgotten. The soldiers had forsaken the barriers.

The Iron Curtain was well and truly breached.

As we drove through the Romanian countryside which we knew so well, the road through every village was lined with waving people. When we stopped for fuel we were surrounded by chatting and excited children and curious adults. We shared some tins of food, but had to make a hasty departure lest we should reach our destination with empty vehicles!

It was early Sunday morning, and our destination was a village near the city of Pitesti. The church in Sibiu had informed us that a new Christian work had been commenced in the village of Badulesti, and that some of them would meet us there for the morning service.

When we arrived, at about 10.30 a.m., the service had been going for an hour. It was held in an unfurnished room at the back of a house belonging to one of the local Christians. We estimated that about fifty people were packed into this small building. Outside, in the open garden, were rows of backless benches for an anticipated overflow congregation.

This new fellowship had commenced the previous February with about twenty baptised believers, or 'repenters', as they are called in Romania. Each week the numbers of new converts were increasing. The work was being overseen by responsible elders from Sibiu.

As the service continued towards noon, people kept coming. They arrived on foot, on bicycles, in horse-drawn carts, and some in 'cars'! One or two had just made it, their engines pouring out smoke; and one was having running repairs to a damaged back axle!

All the while, as the preaching continued, the benches outside were filling up. Groups of people who could not find a seat stood around. No doubt, many wondered what was going on: this was all so new and different! The windows and door had been taken out of the meeting room, so that people who were standing near the entrance could hear the messages.

By mid-day the numbers had swelled to about one hundred. Many of them were children and teenagers. Those outside were divided into two groups. Separate open-air meetings were conducted for them - one for the children and the other for the rest.

When it came my turn to speak in the meeting room the message was translated first into German, and then into Romanian. It was a moving meeting, in every sense! Members of the small congregation kept vacating their seats for newcomers, who insisted on getting inside!

I soon discovered that Romania was not the place to come preaching, if the pre-requisite was a quiet and motionless audience! I had been reared in evangelistic meetings where the preacher requested silence at the end of the service, lest Satan should snatch away the good seed and anxious souls miss salvation - and I have no quarrel with this. It was clear to me, however, that, here in Romania, movement and physical disturbance were no hindrance to the operations of the Holy Spirit. But it took some getting used to! If I had stopped speaking every time there was a distraction, there would have been no message! In the new situation of freedom, people who were unfamiliar with church services had no idea of the normally accepted codes of practice.

I had not spoken for more than fifteen minutes when a man stood up and began to address me in Romanian. As I did not know what he was saying, I sat down. My interpreter responded to him at some length. He eventually sat down, and I was asked to continue!

There was a 'break-time' at the end of the message. It was now one o'clock, and they announced that the meeting would resume at one-thirty. By my calculation, it had already lasted three and a half hours!

I was anxious to know from Fritz what the man who had interrupted had said. A rough translation was, "This is the first time I have been here. It is the first time that I have heard this message. This is what I need. How do I become a repenter?" I knew that Christians in Romania are called 'repenters'. It has the same derogatory meaning as the original word 'Christian', used by the sceptics at Antioch, and recorded in the Acts of the Apostles.

In response to the man's enquiry, Fritz had explained the necessity to repent and take a step of faith, by acknowledging Jesus as his Saviour and Lord. He was asked to resume his seat and to wait behind at the end of the service for a fuller explanation and prayer.

In fact, at the break-time, there were fourteen people standing in a circle in the meeting room. Most were weeping; all wanted to confess their belief and trust in Jesus as their Saviour.

Lunch?!

I was really hungry, but there was no sign of food. People stood about in groups, discussing the Scriptures, asking questions about the messages and exchanging greetings. Everything, but food!

We decided to open the van. The driver reminded us that he had two boxes of bananas. When we bought them in Germany they were under-ripe, now they were just ready for eating. We began to give them out. The children came in great haste; the adults, rather embarrassed, hung back.

For some, it was their very first banana!

One little fellow tried to bite the skin. Another gave it to his mother to put into her bag. He wanted to share it with somebody at home! Soon the two boxes were empty!

The next course was sweets and chocolate. What luxury! We had to severely ration the individual portions, or we wouldn't have had enough to go round.

We resumed the meeting - or meetings - one indoors and the other outside. After praise, prayer, and closing messages, we concluded at about three o'clock. Nobody was in any hurry home, but gradually most filtered away, after what had been the experience of a lifetime. Some were rejoicing in new life in Christ, others were contemplating what they had heard.

"Yes, we will come back. When is the next meeting?", they asked.

"Maranatha!" "Maranatha!", the Christians echoed.

Eventually our numbers were depleted to around twenty. As in Czechoslovakia, the meeting room was transformed into a dining room, and we all sat down to a Romanian meal of bread, sheep's cheese, sausage, and a variety of artistically decorated mayonnaise dishes.

What a happy occasion! Frequently I had to hold back the tears. My generation of Northern Ireland Christians had never experienced anything like this.

This was revival time!

After prayer, we said our good-byes. Escorted by our Sibiu friends, our three cars turned north. We arrived in Sibiu about seven o'clock and were driven to the evening meeting, which had already commenced at six o'clock. It was packed! Every seat and sitting space was taken, and about fifty were crowded into the vestibule and around the door.

It was preaching time all over again. Nobody seemed to take into account that preachers get tired! However, it was my experience that *"His strength was made perfect in weakness"*.

CHAPTER XXIV

"With God All Things Are Possible"

I returned to Badulesti in August of 1990. The friend, at whose house the church met, took me into the adjoining field. He swept his hand around the immediate area where we were standing, and said "We are going to build a Prayer House here"!

"When do you hope to start building?" I enquired.

"In two months' time", he replied; and then continued "It will be a big one!"

"Big?", I said.

"Yes", he replied, with another flourish of his arm, "for about five hundred people!"

"You've a very small number at the moment. Are you sure you're wise to build it so large?"

He smiled and said, "God is going to bring many people!".

"This will cost a lot of money", I ventured, trying to temper his enthusiasm with realism.

"I know", he enthused, "but we will do all the work ourselves, and it will cost less."

"Where will you get the money from?", I continued. He smiled ruefully, and said quietly "From God!".

There was no answer to that.

It so happened that I had some funds in my lodgings in Sibiu, and I instantly felt that I should contribute to this project. I could not help thinking of our Lord's words, *"I have not seen so great faith ..."*.

Badulesti is not really a village, it is more a disparate scattering of houses and small farm holdings. Between August and the following March the congregation had grown to about sixty baptised believers. A building for five hundred seemed to me to be overdoing it, but I kept my counsel. I had the feeling that this figure would be beyond their reach. Before leaving that evening, I said to my friend Dani, "I have some money in Sibiu. I will leave it for you, and perhaps the next time you are travelling there you could collect it."

"I'll come for it tomorrow", he said.

"But that's a long way for you to come", I replied.

"It's all right. It's not a problem", he responded. So we arranged a suitable time for him to call the following day. Before we left the site of this proposed building, a few of us stood in a small circle and, with bowed heads, commended the project and the faith of this infant church to her Head in heaven. We then said our farewells and left.

The next day, at the appointed time, I handed an envelope to Dani, and received his signature that he had been given help for the building project. A photograph was taken to mark the event! He returned south, a happy man. They had implicit trust in God, and He had begun to answer their prayers.

When I returned nine months later I had to catch my breath. I just could not believe that I was looking at a solidly constructed building, with the roof already in place! And they were not in debt. Their God was supplying their need, answering their prayers, and blessing their faith. The number in the fellowship was now approaching one hundred.

"Please let me know when the opening of the new building is to take place. I would love to be present, if at all possible", I said to Dani.

"Yes we will", he replied. "We think it will be within a few months."

Back in Ireland, whilst I was planning my next visit to coincide with the opening of the Badulesti Prayer House, I received a firm date. Then a phone call came, to say that it had been put back for a few weeks. So I was given a new date; and was just about to book my ticket when I heard that it had been changed again! It would definitely be in three weeks' time. This is Romania!! I readjusted my booking, and set out in anticipation of being in Badulesti on the all-important date.

On arrival, however, I was unapologetically told that the opening would not be for some weeks! They were encountering some last minute difficulties. So, after all my planning, I was going to miss the opening! I protested mildly, and went through the changes of date with some emphasis; but nothing could be done about it. "Anyway", I reflected, "why should I make demands on these dear people? Was it not truly marvellous that they had accomplished what they had, in such a relatively short time!"

When I returned home I sent a little note of congratulations to Dani, and assured him that they would all be in my thoughts and prayers. The Big Event took place, and a short time later I received a letter from Costica Morariu, dated 21st September 1992. It contained the following paragraph:

"Badulesti.   Last Sunday we had the opening (more outside than in), and we celebrated it with joy. The last to speak was YOU. One of the speakers was preaching about David, and the way he gathered all for God's Temple, but never got a chance to open it. So, I read your letter from the "David of Badulesti!" Much joy ...... Next week, we will celebrate a wedding in the new building. By His grace we will be present. At the same time, we will start the catechism for the new candidates for baptism. The people from Badulesti, together with a number from our church, evangelised in a village not too far from them and sixteen came to know Christ. We managed to hire a sort of room for them. Every week believers from Badulesti lead their meetings ...."

Another new testimony was being established in a needy area, to the glory of God; and, already, they were reaching out to others.

CHAPTER XXV

The Kingdom Of Nicolae

I t is said that unwritten history has a short memory. It must also be said that the totality of repressive events in Eastern Europe in the past seventy years is too great and too severe for history adequately to record.

As we met the Christians in their homes and churches, there was no sense of bitterness, recrimination, or a longing for retaliation. Frustration, yes; but no compulsive rush to detail things as they really were. Anyhow, many, many of the events perpetrated by the government, they knew nothing about.

The most powerful comment on their plight, to some friends and me, was made without words. It happened in Romania's White House - Ceaucescu's unfinished palace in Bucharest.

We joined a never ending stream of sullen-eyed Romanians, as they silently snaked their way through the six opulent Halls of Culture. They observed the larger than life carved wooden double doors, the fluted and ornamented marble pillars, the gold-plated radiators, the elaborate crystal chandeliers, and the wall-to-wall woven carpets. (I am told the weight of one carpet is six tonnes!) All of this stunned the moving masses into an uneasy silence, and me to righteous anger.

Many thousands of craftsmen were conscripted to produce this massive structure, and some of them never lived to tell the tale. They were conveniently liquidated, lest reports of this most secret of all projects would leak out to a starving public. Our guide showed us one section of the great hall where the marble had not been to the President's liking, so in a fit of rage he ordered it to be ripped out and replaced. The cost must have been enormous.

Indignation, intermingled with deep sorrow, filled my heart on that two-hour excursion into the Kingdom of Nicolae and Elena Ceaucescu. I was only a visitor, regarded by the guide as a tourist from the West; but the people all around me were seeing and feeling this experience against the background of their squalid lifestyle, imposed upon them by these self-exalted gods.

The population of this beautiful land had watched the historic centres of their cities being bull-dozed; and, even more extraordinary, their villages systematically destroyed. Ceaucescu's evil scheme was to demolish almost eight thousand traditional villages, history written into their very walls, and by the end of the century replace them with concrete agro-industrial complexes.

As the sightseers surveyed the massive grandeur of their late President's twisted dreams, they would reflect that their country was denied basic medical services. Even Emergency services were not available to people over sixty years of age - they were not worth bothering about! The birth of a child was not registered until it was about six months old. If it died before that, it was not recorded! People stood in queues all night for food which may not even materialise by morning. Repeated electricity cuts, in sub-zero temperatures, sent people to an early bed, fully clothed, and hungry.

Unknown to the Romanian people, there were overcrowded, horrendous orphanages and old-age institutions, that subsequently earned the title "Europe's foul basement".

What they also did not know was that their President had several Swiss bank accounts, and owned numerous summer residences on the Black Sea, and shooting lodges in carefully guarded beauty spots in the Romanian mountains!

In the mid 1980's, at the height of the crisis, a Western visitor noticed several large foreign registered trucks.

"Why are there so many foreign trucks here?", he asked.

His Romanian friend replied, "They have come to take away our food!".

Although Romania had some of the best agricultural land in Europe - "The Bread Basket of Europe", they called it - the people were starving. In order to pay off the country's high foreign debt, the authorities imposed this evil exportation policy. Against this background of political tyranny and economic sabotage, the true church of God worshipped their Lord and preached the gospel of repentance and salvation through the blood of His cross.

Despite the reluctant recognition given to the Evangelical churches by the State, there was a systematic brain-washing, even of the strongest Christians. The majority physically survived this ordeal, but many were broken by it. Under the severest of personal pressures, some compromised their position of loyalty to the Lord and the church. Sadly, some did it for favours bestowed by their Communist masters. But the majority were staunch in their stand for the Lord.

I remember a meeting of the elders, called to denounce a fellow elder because he had co-operated with the Securitate. Without fully comprehending the true nature of the meeting, a friend and I were asked to attend. The most vocal spokesman was a young man in his thirties, who had apparently just come to prominence in the months following the Revolution. He wanted the 'offending' elder not only stripped of his authority, but excommunicated!

"What do you think?", he asked me.

My immediate response was, *"There is forgiveness with the Lord, that he may be feared"*.

As I spoke I could see in my mind's eye a framed picture in a room in Bucharest. It depicted a large lake, and a post had been driven into the lake with a signboard on it, with words in Romanian which I did not understand. At the bottom of the picture was a familiar Scripture text, quoting from Micah 7:19, *"Thou wilt cast all their sins into the depths of the sea"*. They told me that the notice on the signboard read "NO FISHING"!

The pressure on Evangelical church leaders had been immense. Psychological, as well as physical torture was not uncommon. Nothing was outside the agenda of Romania's ruthless rulers: imprisonment and, in extreme cases, even death.

I have referred to the leading elders representing the Brethren churches who were arrested, tried, and imprisoned for the possession of Bibles. In the summer of 1993 I drove past the prison where they had been confined. My friend Mircea, a passenger in the car, had been one of those prisoners. "How do you feel?", I asked him as we passed by.

"I still have fear in my heart", came the quiet reply.

As with all God's persecuted and martyred children of every generation, the maxim holds good: "Only eternity will reveal the true cost paid in human suffering by the faithful followers of a rejected Master".

All of this and more was flooding my mind as our visit to Ceaucescu's Palace came to an end. When we arrived at the Exit door we thanked our guide. I said to him, by interpretation, "Can you come with us to our car? I have a present for you". His face broke into a smile.

As we walked down the path, my Scottish friend said to him, "This is a marvellous palace, but I know a better one! It is called 'the house of many mansions'. It's in heaven!"

"I know", said the guide, with an even broader smile. "I'm a member of the Baptist church!"

What a shock! We stopped, and each of us in turn embraced this young Christian who had survived the rigors of the Communist regime. When we reached our vehicle we filled a plastic bag with food items. He was so pleased! One day we will meet again. If not in Romania, then certainly in the heavenly mansions.

CHAPTER XXVI

Coming To Terms With Changed Conditions

W hen we arrived at the church in Sibiu, what a change there too! The atmosphere in the meeting was totally transformed. There was a brightness, and an obvious sense of occasion. We had liberty to say whatever we wanted. It was a heart-warming experience to join in thanksgiving and praise for FREEDOM.

All the cowered coming and going had vanished. After the meeting, the street thronged with elated and chattering people, embracing, laughing, and weeping tears of irrepressible joy!

As in Sibiu, so elsewhere. Christians congregated freely in the streets after the services. A sense of excitement pervaded, as everyone emotionally voiced thanks to God for deliverance and freedom.

In the villages, the playing of a guitar or taped music was the rallying signal for many children and curious adults. There was no problem in gathering a crowd. Many churches took full advantage of every opportunity to make known the message of the cross:

Salvation, not through a church or creed, but through the blood of Jesus the Son of God.

On Sunday afternoons, and occasionally on an arranged week-night, the Christians would hire cultural halls for a special evange-listic meeting. Someone would announce the meeting through a home-made megaphone, and the villagers would come. There was a sense of something eventful happening, and a pressing curiosity about anything new.

These halls were usually like the black hole of Calcutta! There was very little light, they were dirty, and smelt pungent. We arrived at one such building on an extremely hot Sunday afternoon. The village street adjacent to the hall was alive with people.

"Why are they not inside?", I enquired.

"Because it's already full!", was the reply.

We entered the rear of the theatre-type auditorium, and walked down a sloping floor to the stage. Coming out of the bright sunlight, one would have needed a torch to negotiate the steps down the side of the building. I was aware of people - lots of them! There was not a vacant place. I calculated that there must have been over three hundred people sitting crammed together on backless benches. There were no windows, and the majority of the one-tube fluorescent lights were not working.

I reached the front and climbed on to the stage, where I was greeted by the Christian workers who had organised this special event. They said that the Orthodox priest was very angry at what was taking place, and had warned his congregation to stay away. From the numbers present, inside and outside the building, it appeared his words had fallen on deaf ears.

After a brief introduction I was asked to preach. "As far as I know," said the Chairman, "there are no believers in the congregation! This is the first time they will have heard the gospel preached."

What a challenge! What an awesome responsibility!

There was rapt attention during the forty-five minute message. As I became accustomed to the dim light, I could make out rows of men, women and children, with their eyes fastened on the translator. There was a marvellous release of the Spirit and a sense of eternity in that meeting. When I concluded, one of Romania's best evangelists began to preach. I didn't need to understand his message because it was obvious that he was speaking with authority and power. People began to weep. There was unease and movement among the congregation as the impact of the message and the convicting power of the Holy Spirit moved among them.

The evangelist gave an invitation to those who wanted more information, or any who wanted to trust Jesus as Saviour and Lord, to wait behind. Many did. Bibles and tracts were distributed, and it almost became a stampede, to the point of being dangerous, so eager were they to obtain the Scriptures or the tracts.

As we left that village, my lasting memory is of clusters of people all along the dusty road, waving and smiling their good-byes. Many shouted "Come back soon!".

We drove directly to another village church, and found their meeting room packed to overflowing. Men, women and children, some in arms, stood around the open doors and windows. We joined the congregation in their singing, and then I was invited to preach. "We have about one hour", Costica told me, "then we must drive to Sibiu for the evening service"!

As soon as I finished the message we asked to be excused, and left. In half an hour we were driving through Sibiu!

By this time I was quite exhausted.

"Costica", I pleaded, "can this be a short message? This will the fourth time today that I have preached!"

He smiled, and said "we shall see! They are expecting you and want to hear your message! Preach the same message again here!", he encouraged me. "They need to hear this word from the Lord."

It was at times like these that I had to draw deeply not only on my physical resources, but on the spiritual ones as well. I never felt too comfortable, preaching the same message twice on the same day. But that day I had no choice!

I can testify that on the numerous occasions when, in different meetings, I set out to repeat a message, it never came out the same way! The Lord came and stood with me; and reserves of energy, forgotten themes, and spiritual power came quickly, to convict sinners and challenge saints.

It was nine o'clock before we returned home, and ten o'clock before we sat down to eat. My hosts had invited guests in to enjoy the fellowship. They wanted to hear about my family, my church, Irelanda du Nord, and much more; it was a real endurance test! The room in which we ate was my bedroom. Several times I looked longingly at the neat pile of folded bedclothes on the couch, but it was past midnight before my desire was realised!

Over the succeeding years, in these and many other locations, the same Sunday format has been repeated. Hunger for the Word of God was insatiable. At every meeting men and women responded to the call of salvation. Tears of joy flowed freely, flowers were exchanged, new Bibles handed out, accompanied by warm embraces and more and more Maranathas and Hallelujahs!

CHAPTER XXVII

Doina

I t was in August 1990 that Doina travelled back to Northern Ireland with me. She had been awarded a scholarship to the Belfast Bible College, to do a one-year course in Biblical Studies, Greek and Hebrew, and to study for the Cambridge University Level 2 English examination.

Three months previously I had written to her:

"Sit down, Doina, before you read this", I began. "The Belfast Bible College Registrar has asked me if I know a Romanian Christian who would benefit from a one year course." I described it to her, and enclosed a College brochure. "I have felt very strongly that you are the person to take up this offer, and I realise it will mean you leaving your home, family and your work." At that time she was employed as a dental technician in the local hospital. "It will be a very big decision for you to make", I continued, "but pray about it, talk it over with your family and someone in the church, and let me know your decision within a month!"

Two weeks later I had a telephone call. "This is Doina. The answer is Yes! What do I have to do?"

I told her that I would send an application form, and she should apply for a passport and visa.

"I will be coming to Romania, God willing, in August, and you could come back to Ireland with me. This would make it easier for you to make the break from home, and it will also reassure your family that you are in 'good hands'!"

I duly arrived in Sibiu, only to discover that Doina did not have her visa - despite numerous phone calls to the British Embassy in Bucharest.

After weeks of frustration, she was granted a one-year visa. For the two days prior to flying out of Romania, she and I had camped on the door step of the British Embassy in Bucharest. We were shunted from pillar to post! Time was running out. All kinds of thoughts were racing through my mind. What if she didn't get a visa? Her ticket had been purchased. She had said a tearful farewell to her loved ones up north in Sibiu. It really was a nail-biting experience. We prayed often, in short, intense cries to the Lord.

In the end the answer came. The visa was issued at 6.00 p.m. (two hours after the Embassy closed!) on the evening before our departure. We stood on the footway, hugged each other, and thanked the Lord for solving the problem.

Next morning she was strapped into her seat on an ageing DC9 of TAROM airlines, en route to London and Belfast.

I had spent many hours trying to condition her to the problems she would encounter in Ireland. "Homesickness, bewilderment and loneliness will sometimes be your companions, Doina", I said gently, as I tried to explain what culture shock was. "But you will have happy and precious times too, and they will far outweigh the difficulties!", I consoled her.

"Don't worry", she kept repeating, "I'll be all right." We both knew that the Lord had opened this marvellous door of opportunity; but that didn't mean she would have no problems!

In fact, the whole experience proved to be more traumatic for her, and for those who tried to comfort and encourage her, than we had expected. It was her fervent desire to be better equipped to serve the Lord among children and young people in the new Romania, and it was this that motivated her to stay the course and successfully complete it.

As we rose above the clouds, floating below us like gigantic balls of cotton wool, many on their first trip would have likened it to fairyland. To Doina, it was "like being near to heaven". After a trouble free flight we landed at No. 2 Terminal, London Heathrow, and followed the carpeted walkway to the baggage carousel.

"Look at these carpets! Everything is so clean!", she chattered on and on!

A child in a new world! We waited to claim our baggage. The carousel went round and round until every case had gone. "Where's ours?", we both exclaimed simultaneously.

Back in Bucharest! "It will be on the next aircraft", explained the attendant, apologetically. "Give me your names and address, and it will be delivered to you!"

"We are going to Belfast", I said, "on the next plane."

"That doesn't matter. Your luggage will be forwarded as soon as possible", he reassured us. So there we were! I was all right, but

Doina had only her hand luggage and nothing else! What an introduction to a strange land! There was no panic, however. The Lord gave us peace in our hearts. On the Belfast-bound journey we thanked God together for His presence, and simply asked that the luggage would arrive safely, and for success to accompany my young friend's mission.

Early in her stay in Dundonald we walked in the countryside to the top of the hill above our home and sat down on a wall, overlooking the city of Belfast.

"Look at all those lights - so many!", she whispered. Then she fell silent.

Georgie and I exchanged knowing glances, as we noticed that she was fighting back the tears.

The battle had begun.

CHAPTER XXVIII

If Mummy Could See Me Now!

The baggage duly arrived, at different times, some days later. It had been tampered with, but nothing was missing.

Doina stayed with us for the following two weeks.

That first fortnight in our home was a happy but unnerving experience, as Doina tried to come to terms with everything that was alien to her knowledge and culture. She had no interest in shops or sightseeing. Our best times were when we read the Scriptures together and prayed. Night after night her consolation was found in deep communication with her Lord. Then there were unpredictable times; like when she ate a layer of a box of chocolates, one after the other!

"Do you know you've just eaten a day's wages?", I quipped.

"I'm sorry!", she whispered. "You know, in our country, when we get some luxury like this we eat it all at once. We feel compelled to eat it."

Her first visit to the local supermarket was quite upsetting. She went in, not very far, looked around, and said "I don't like it in here!".

"What's wrong, Doina?", I asked reassuringly.

"When will these shelves all be empty?", she enquired.

I told her that as people bought food the shelves were filled up again. "They are always pretty full", I replied.

"That means there is more food, than people to eat it?", she queried.

"I suppose that's right, if you put it like that!" I said, rather light-heartedly.

She said no more and quickly made for the exit door. I knew what she was thinking. Their supermarket shelves at that time were empty, or nearly empty. They had some money, but there was little or nothing to buy. On the way home she volunteered, "If my mummy could see me now she wouldn't believe it!".

In time she successfully overcame the pain barrier and would shop happily with us; but she was never really interested in buying anything for herself. On one visit to the store we had bought a few items and packed them into two plastic bags. Doina wanted to carry one. As she emerged through the revolving doors she began to gleefully swing the bag, shoulder high! "Stop it," I shouted, "the handles will break!"

"This is the wave offering!", she retorted unabashed, with a twinkle in her eye. To her all things were woven around an inner spiritual life.

26th December, Boxing Day, was a special day. It was her 21st birthday; and the first time in her young life that she had received birthday cards and a cake! She found it difficult to come to terms with the situation.

Her year at the college ended with top marks in Greek and Hebrew; and a B grade in the Cambridge English exam, which she considered to be a real achievement. And so it was!

During her stay in Ireland we grew to love her, and she found it second nature to call us Mum and Dad. We were, and still are proud to look on her as our adopted daughter.

After a number of months back at home in Romania, we received the following written contribution of her thoughts about Northern Ireland. Apart from some minor modifications to ease the flow of the English, it remains as I received it:

GOD AND I

God gave me grace to count the stars
In a land I'd never seen before.
They say it's the land
Where most of the neighbours hate each other;
I found it a land
Where people's hearts were warm and open.

God gave me wisdom
To speak a language my mother never taught me,
A desire to give myself to Him,
And a fear I never had before, to revere Him.

He allowed me to see with my own eyes
A land, a dream come true.
He gave me grace to grasp the meaning of so many sayings
Which did not belong to my world.

He gave me mothers and fathers I did not ask for,
Friends I did not hope to have,
Privileges of princesses only.
Joy in shared tears.

Another Christmas dinner!
With presents just for me.
He wanted me to grow wiser.
When I cried,
He told me His grace would be enough.

He sent times when separation hurt,
When days and nights were long,
And prayer could not find the words.

The schoolgirl became a strong woman.
The child in me grew older,
The prayer more powerful,
Love found new dimensions,
Words for Him came from my mouth in praise.

Those who saw me at the start,
Watched me in between,
Admired me at the end!

But nobody really understood
The struggle,
The inner beauty
Of that work of revealing treasures
In a jar of clay.

God alone knew what I was to be and do.
He alone knows what it takes to make me
Be and do.
He alone has the power to work it through -
Power for my weakness.

I can only believe, trust and accept
That every next second
God and I will be together.
In that, I rest content.
For He has promised to finish
His work in me.

August 1992.

CHAPTER XXIX

"Fantastic!"

"Fantastic!" he exclaimed, as he arose from a crouching position in the centre of a road in County Down.

"Fantastic!"

The speaker who marvelled so much at the common "cats-eye" was my friend Bernard. He and his friend Mircea, whom I have already referred to, were Christian leaders from two different areas in Romania. They had been invited to visit Britain, and were now visiting us and calling with some other friends in Northern Ireland. I had stayed in their homes on a number of occasions, and it was a pleasure to return the great kindness they had shown to me.

"There's a lesson you could preach from the cat's-eye!", I said. "The inventor died in poverty, but those who produced and manufactured his invention became millionaires!"

Before we drove off, we thought together of the One who had become poor to produce the Divine invention of salvation, and through whose poverty we had become rich.

"Better than millionaires!", they echoed.

"Brothers in Christ and *'blessed with all spiritual blessings in the heavenly places in Christ Jesus'"*, I added.

On that occasion I recounted the words of a mutual friend in Romania who, when under intense questioning from the Securitate, was asked by the policeman, "How is it that you invite foreigners, complete strangers, to your home and to your church? What is the point of bringing them here?"

"Strangers! Foreigners!", my friend exclaimed. "They are not! They are *'fellow citizens of the household of faith'*! We have thousands, perhaps millions, of spiritual brothers and sisters all over the world. We may never see them or know them personally in this life; but we know they are there. These people, who travel many miles to see us, bring us greetings from them. This is the result of our faith, and you cannot destroy it!"

Now in Great Britain and Northern Ireland, these friends were meeting and having fellowship with Christians from all walks of life. Different dialects and customs, but all one in the Body of Christ. The dying embers of Communism were strewn around in Eastern Europe, but the church of Jesus Christ was a living organism that could not be destroyed.

As we travelled together around Northern Ireland and met in various homes, their eyes would be exploring their new surroundings. I knew what they were thinking: "what luxury these people live in!". Not in a hundred years, could they ever have this standard of living. We did not talk much about our material advantages, but my constant mental comparisons with their situation back home made me more than a little uncomfortable at times.

On the last day of their stay in our home (a conventional, three up-two down, semi-detached house in a quiet residential area on the fringe of Belfast), one of my friends pushed open the door of our downstairs front room. He stepped inside and looked around. There was the traditional three-piece suite and some occasional furniture, pretty standard for a small room.

"What is this?" he asked.

"It's a sitting room", I said.

"What do you use it for?", he enquired.

"Sometimes, when we have friends in, or when someone comes to have a personal talk with me, we use this room."

"But we haven't used it this week!", he continued.

I didn't know how to respond adequately. I knew he was comparing it with his little house, which accommodated his wife and three growing girls. By comparison, for him our house was luxurious - more than we needed.

I reflected on his hospitality when we would arrive, laden with baggage, usually unannounced. We would be welcomed with a smile and warm embrace. The girls would vacate their bedroom for us. In the morning we would share the tiny bathroom, off the equally tiny kitchen. There was an all-in-it-together feeling. In a lighter moment, one of my friends expressed, "You have close fellowship in Romania!".

On my next visit to my friend's house, we were discussing the Scriptures together, and he was also thinking back to his experiences in the West. "You know, my dear brother, I have to be content with my lot here, and with our home and situation! My heart - no! not my heart, my flesh - said to me, that I would like a house and a car like yours. I know it is the flesh, and the Lord tells me that I have to keep it in control."

The conversation ended with his slapping me on the back, and in laughter exclaiming, "My brother, when our heavenly Father said He would make us 'rich', He wasn't talking about houses and cars!".

CHAPTER XXX

You Shall Be My Witnesses

In August 1992, after a two year break, Gerald and I met up again, in the beautiful resort of Busteni, high up in the Bucegi Mountains. The road from Brasov to Ploiesti is like the road from Jerusalem to Jericho - downhill all the way. In typical fashion, road, rail, and river snake their way together among the steeply forested mountain slopes, and through the tourist towns with their mixture of alpine leisure pursuits and down-in-the-heel industrial complexes.

Busteni, one of the major ski and mountain-climbing areas, was the site of a twenty-eight strong Youth camp, organised and run by the Brethren church in Ploiesti, fifty miles further south. The accommodation was in a wooden cabin situated on the east side of the valley, with a spectacular view of the three jagged mountain peaks that dominate the range.

With true-to-form dedication, the workers had been travelling to the site in the evenings and at weekends for months previously, to ensure that it was ready for this very first camp venture. Gerald and I made the numbers up to thirty, so we were billeted out to a local elder's home where we were warmly welcomed. It was a tiny little flat, and someone had obviously vacated their bed on our account.

The topic for the week's study was "The Person and Work of the Holy Spirit". I was responsible for the morning studies on the doctrinal aspects of the subject. These commenced at 9.00 a.m., preceded by lively prayer sessions, and concluded at 1.00 p.m., with two fifteen-minute breaks for refreshments. Gerald had the evening sessions, between 5.00 p.m. and 7.00 p.m., on the practical areas of the Holy Spirit's ministry in the Christian's life.

There was no reference in the programme to games or outdoor activities, and this struck me as odd. In my experience in Camp work over many years, I knew that well organised physical activities were a necessary balance to the times of Bible teaching and discussion. On making enquiries from the leader, I discovered that the times between the studies, other than for eating, were for siesta, study or further discussion! I was always very thankful for this siesta time in the long, busy days that characterised the Romanian visits. We referred to it, much to their amusement, as 'horizontal meditation'!

However, I spent some of the time just gazing at the wonder of God's creation, and I felt a great urge to get these young folk up the mountains by the cable car which was located in Busteni town. I enquired about the cost, time required to complete the round trip, and the logistics of getting thirty people into the cars. My plan was to request that the evening study session on the Wednesday be put back by two hours to allow time for this outing. I was satisfied with the cost - a little under £20 in total. I would have to pay for it, as the campers could not afford it. To them it was a very large amount of money. I discussed the proposal with the leader on Tuesday, and suggested that we keep it a surprise and not announce it until after lunch on Wednesday.

I was quite taken aback at his reaction. He ruled it out completely, saying "We have come here to study the Word, not for recreation. That would be wasting valuable time! And anyway", he concluded after a long pause, "it's too costly. These people wouldn't have the money to pay for such a visit."

We had quite an animated discussion, but I really did want to let these young Romanians have the 'trip of a lifetime', without sacrificing the precious Bible Study time. The leader saw my resolute attitude, and eventually relented, but added that he had to return home for a short visit and would not be going with us. When the announcement of the trip was made, there were suppressed cries of joy.

On the final count, twenty-five of us made the half-hour journey on foot to the cable car ticket office, and arranged to go up in two groups, in two cable cars, with a staggered start of fifteen minutes. The time taken to do the ascent was only twelve minutes.

As we congregated in the waiting area, the young people sang choruses. The building was made of concrete, so the acoustics were superb! There were many other tourists waiting, and suddenly the atmosphere was transformed. Astonished people stood riveted, in wondering silence. The majority would never have heard the name of Jesus being sung so enthusiastically as from these youthful lips. And their faces were shining!

As I talked with Gerald about the impact this was having, a man with a knapsack touched my shoulder, and enquired in English, "You speak English. Are you an American?".

"No", I replied, "I'm Irish - I come from Northern Ireland."

"But", he said, "that is where the bombs go off!"

So for the next ten minutes he peppered me with political questions, which terminated when he suddenly changed tack, and asked, "How is it that you are with these young people in Romania?". Before I got time to answer, he continued, "Do you have money?".

"Yes," I replied, rather bewildered.

"They will steal it", he observed. "You cannot trust them."

I had to disagree: "I can trust this group completely. In fact, they would give me money, if they had it! These young people are REAL Christians", I said, and went on quickly to explain the gospel.

"They sing about Jesus because they have learned that He is the Son of God who died on the cross to bear their sins, and give them eternal life. They have repented. They are true Christians."

"Yes", he said, "I have heard something about a religious revival in Romania."

The conversation was cut short with the arrival of the cable car. We had one exhilarating hour on the summit, taking in the breathtaking panoramic views. The sheer delight of this new experience for the campers was all too evident. We talked about the Creator who was the Sustainer of it all. I told them about the message carved in stone in Northern Ireland's beautiful Tollymore Forest Park, in Newcastle, Co. Down: "Stop, look around, and praise the Name of Him who made it all".

Reluctantly, we retraced our steps to the cable car station, where my friend with the knapsack was waiting for me! He came very close, and said, "I am a High School teacher of history. Would it be possible for you to send me a book of modern English History?".

"I think that would be possible!", I replied. "Let me have your name and address."

Coming even closer, he continued in a nervous voice, "Could I be so bold as to ask for a copy of the Holy Bible? Not your own, but another one - would that be possible?" I really was taken aback at the directness and sincerity of the question. I told him I didn't have a spare Bible with me, but that I could arrange to send him one on my return home. He was delighted with that.

As we descended I remarked to Gerald, "This man wants a Bible. He has given me his name and address, so I've promised to send him one."

"I have one in my case", he replied. "If he has time to come to where we are staying, he can have it!"

When I communicated this message to my Schoolteacher friend, he said with enthusiasm, "Yes, I have time. My mother is with me, but we must wait for an hour before we get our train to Bucharest."

On our descent we made our way the short distance to where we were lodging. As we went, I thought to myself "How good of the Lord to have given us this place to stay, so close to the cable car!". When Gerald emerged with the Bible, he remarked as he handed it to him, with a broad smile, "This is a copy of the Word of God. May He bless your reading of it!"

I can still vividly see this man clutching the Bible, with a tender firmness. With tears, he gratefully said, "Thank you! This is the greatest day of my life". So we parted. The following year I was able to pass on a History book through his wife, while he was teaching at school. I often wonder what change the Bible made to his life.

That evening in the camp meeting, Gerald's subject was "The Power of the Holy Spirit in Witness". He recalled the afternoon's witness in song to the many who listened, and referred to the history teacher from Bucharest who, because of it, went home with a copy of the Scriptures. He emphasised that there was no telling what the Lord would do in lives that were open and ready for the Holy Spirit to operate. The young folk were thrilled, and I noticed that the leader was distinctly uneasy.

Gerald continued, "When I was packing my case, I put in the Bible thinking that somebody might be glad to have it. Then, as my case was too full, I took it out, along with some other items and closed up the case. I looked at the Bible and decided that I must take it. Now I know the reason why!"

As we were leaving the camp site to go to our lodgings, the leader quietly said to me, "I'm sorry, Drew, I didn't properly understand. Next year you must come back and we will all go up the mountain again!"

So far that desire remains unfulfilled.

CHAPTER XXXI

Breaking New Ground

All through the autumn, as I recounted experiences of God's presence and power in Romania, I was always careful to share the necessity of being ready to publicly witness for the Lord. The cable car experience had been a salutary lesson to me, and provided an apt illustration of how spiritual preparedness can be easily transformed into actual and visible blessing.

Towards the end of the year I received a letter from one of the leading Christian workers. In his view, 1992 had been a particularly productive year in gospel outreach. The euphoria immediately following the Revolution was dying down, but the appetite for the Word of God and the message of salvation was undiminished. The large established churches were beginning to look to surrounding towns and villages where there were many possibilities for planting new local fellowships. But the enthusiasm had to be tempered with reality - the lack of suitable accommodation and no finance to provide anything better.

I was familiar with the substantial building programme which was under way in many parts of the country. This was particularly

178 Joy In Shared Tears

so in the area around Ploiesti, a city north of Bucharest with a population of 300,000, where there was a local church of some twelve hundred people with a vigorous outreach to the surrounding community.

The extended, nondescript house which they used could accommodate only five hundred people at a time, so they were in the process of constructing a large hexagonal building in a central location in Ploiesti which would hold eight hundred people. This would enable them to divide the congregation between the old and the new buildings. In addition, there were at least twelve new halls planned, or already under construction, within a twenty-five mile radius of the city.

The Christians living in these villages in Ceaucescu's time commuted to one of the few officially registered churches in a central location in Ploiesti. Now in freedom, they wanted their own building in the village, for fellowship and as a centre of gospel witness. It was not uncommon to have twenty to thirty people gathered in the room of a private home, most of whom had been converted in the previous six to twelve months!

To them, the Scriptures were a new book. The hymns and tunes were unknown, but the Word of God was having its effect. Lives were being changed. Public confession of Jesus as Lord, in immersion baptism, was common, and the simple gathering for corporate prayer, worship and Breaking of Bread was, for them, a completely new way of life.

In general, the new buildings in the villages were neither large nor ostentatious, but they met the need and were lights in dark places. Most of them were built like the pyramids: all available labour was put to work! Men, women, children all worked together as craftsmen, handymen and labourers.

Late one Saturday afternoon I saw a line of young women passing building blocks from one to the other, and up ladders to the scaffolding! Mature women, some bordering on elderly, were mixing lime mortar! They worked every weekend and in the evenings. No task masters were needed because, like Nehemiah, *"everybody had a mind to work"*. They set to the work, and did it willingly for the glory of the Lord who had saved them. It was a powerful public testimony.

It would be wrong to give the impression that all this took place without any difficulties. Satan was always present, in some form, to hinder the work; but, unlike the walls of Jerusalem, the work did not stop because of discouragement or opposition. There were hold-ups, sometimes for months, due to inclement weather or the lack of funds. To the credit of all concerned, the building projects commenced in the 1992 era have been completed, or substantially so.

By early 1994 - less than five years after the Revolution - it was estimated that the number of Brethren churches had increased from under three hundred to almost six hundred, and the number of believers rose from approximately 25,000 to 70,000! By any standards, even those of past Revivals, it was a remarkable work of the Holy Spirit.

The Baptist and Pentecostal churches were also expanding. Before the Revolution, these churches had constituted the mainstream of independent evangelical witness. However, within the Romanian Orthodox Church, there was a large number of born again people, called 'The Lord's Army'. Though very much in the minority, they witnessed quietly within the Orthodox system, and were known to the State Authorities for their profession of faith.

As in all sections of the true church, there were doctrinal differences and preferences; but these were kept within bounds, due to the restrictive system imposed by the Communist government. Now, in freedom, these differences began to surface, and they were encouraged by an impetus from the West. Preachers and teachers of all shades of evangelical opinion were landing on the doorsteps of both new and established churches, proclaiming that theirs was the right way! A few break-off groups were established under a variety of names, and there was much confusion among leaders and elders. However, the saving work of the Lord continued unabated.

I was told there were two dominant features that would affect the future direction of the local churches. In the first place, the political system before the Revolution had done the thinking for the people, and when freedom came they had to begin to think and make decisions for themselves. This proved to be a painful process, in both secular and spiritual matters. It was not easy, particularly, for the older generations. The younger folk were more open to different teaching and were prepared to discuss other points of view, testing what they heard against Scripture.

The second factor was the expansion of doctrine and the deepening of Biblical knowledge, due to the ever-increasing distribution of Christian literature, and this began to have a major effect on the leadership of the churches. For almost fifty years believers had been deprived of study aids. They were shut up to the Lord and the Scriptures. Any doctrinal literature that had existed in the 1930's was hard to find.

During the Ceaucescu years, the church's main messages were exhortation and encouragement. The gospel was preached, it is true, and baptism by immersion was practised by the majority. The Breaking of Bread and prayer were central features of worship, but life was often fraught with uncertainties. Leading elders were arrested, some just disappeared. Many prominent Christians were leaned upon by the Securitate to force them to compromise and co-operate. There were threats to close meeting places, and disperse congregations. Altogether it was hard, very hard. Threats - some veiled, and some quite open - were a common feature of everyday life.

It is not surprising, therefore, that when the church met they had clear objectives. These ministries of exhortation and encouragement ranged across their prayer life, their worship, and their associations in the world. Each crisis brought with it a new sense of urgency, and emergency prayer meetings often took place. Fasting was a common and precious ministry exercised by many.

"Keep going on!"

"Endure hardness, as a good soldier of Jesus Christ." (2 Timothy 2:3)

"Fight the good fight of faith!" (1 Timothy 6:12)

These messages were reinforced week by week.

There was also a heightened expectation of the Lord's return. I have already referred to their watchword, *"Maranatha!"* (the Lord is coming!). The Lord had promised to return to deliver His people; and He had promised to come quickly. As far as they were concerned, He couldn't come soon enough!

These uncomplicated messages of Scripture were the life-blood of the Romanian Christians. Their experiences of God and His Word were a way of life, not just something to be believed as an academic exercise. While I believe this simplicity of faith still persists, it has been built upon by a plethora of doctrinal teachings. This has given a new dimension to their worship and witness, but in some cases it has caused difficulty.

On a recent visit I had the opportunity of browsing in a local elder's book case. I found ten indexed, loose-leaf notebooks, the evidence of intense Bible study. It was the result of a seven-year course with an American organisation called Bible Education by Extension (B.E.E.). This work, carried on in very difficult and dangerous conditions, has paid off.

The notes which I saw covered topics like Creation, Sin, Redemption, and many more doctrinal themes. There were studies in Nehemiah, Psalms, Ezekiel, and Revelation. I was quite taken aback by the range of material. And it was all in copper-plate handwriting! I tried to assess the hours of study that were involved, sometimes without heat, in intense cold, behind locked doors, and travelling to venues at night for fellowship around the Word of God.

Sometimes they went in the midnight train to Bucharest - a journey of five hours - standing all the way in the packed corridors. When they arrived they would go to a secret apartment, and the whole of the day would be devoted to intensive study, evaluation of their work, or an examination. During the night they would return home, and go straight to work.

As I turned page after page I realised that I was looking into the soul of a dear friend and beloved brother in the Lord, and I felt ashamed! I had no right to invade this private domain.

I had come from a place of high privilege, where there were study aids in abundance, and freedom to use them. Every possible encouragement was given to be a workman who would not be ashamed, because he could rightly divide the word of truth (2 Timothy 2:15) . But what did I really know about the Psalms, I asked myself - analytically, or synthetically? What about Ezekiel or, for that matter, Revelation? That day, alone in that little room with the notebooks and a varied amount of new publications recently come from the West, I learned some valuable lessons; one of the principal ones being that I should never underestimate the work of God in their lives. Men who had thus hazarded their lives for the gospel were worthy of great respect. As a visitor in their country, I felt the Scriptural injunction was very apt: *"esteem them very highly in love for their work's sake"* (1 Thess. 5:13).

CHAPTER XXXII

"I Will Build My Church"

About the time of the opening of the Badulesti Assembly I received news of other outreaches in Southern Transylvania and its sister province of Oltenia, lying still further to the south. The following are verbatim excerpts from some of those letters, written by a friend who was endeavouring to help and encourage:

"We had the opportunity to hold an evangelistic meeting at **PETROSANI**, a town in the valley of Jiu, about one hundred kilometres from Sibiu. The coal miners who went to Bucharest to protest came from this area. The meeting was held in a Cultural Hall - many were there, and almost thirty wanted to know Christ as their Saviour. We just feel sorry because there was no fellowship in the area. The few believers there meet in a very small room. The Lord has strengthened us to believe that the work will grow."

"Another evangelistic meeting in a village near **ALBA** - no Christian testimony. In old times elders from our churches were stoned when they tried to bring the gospel. We prayed with the members of our own Assembly, and managed to hire the Cultural Hall. Almost one hundred and fifty villagers were present. We preached and in spite of the hostility (men did not want to take their hats off!), God moved them, and we could see them weeping ... At the end they had one desire, "Please come back". The village is now split into two; some of them would do anything to have us. Pray for **DOSTAT** (the name of the village)."

"In Oltenia, a county in the southern area of Romania, in a village towards **CRAIOVA** - a fairly large one - the priest had all our posters torn down. He had a crowd of men and women try to stop the others coming to the hall. More than that - he had drunkards set up to spoil our meeting. But we had an audience of eighty people, people who had never heard this word 'Bible'.

Sixty kilometres from here, we tried in another village to find Christians - we couldn't find any. We had to pay 7,000 lei to the Director of the Cultural Hall - the priest's cousin! The gospel was preached with power, many were weeping and they asked us to come down again. The Director promised to rent the hall to us. We have this village and another strong Communist town in our future plans. We will advertise in the local newspapers concerning the next meetings."

"In **PITESTI** (the city where I forced Gerald to buy the meal that caused my sickness!), last Sunday we had the opening of a new Assembly. It looked an "intellectual" meeting as they have ten medical doctors among them!

We couldn't afford to buy a place for the building of a new church; the prices were too high. (Anyway it takes a lot of time for such a big project!) So we decided to get a two-roomed apartment in a block of flats. It is already crowded. We will start to build a simple house eventually."

SCHITU GOLESTI

"Lack of workers. In spite of the coming bad weather, we'll have somehow to visit them very often. Many unbelievers turn up to church."

CALIMANESTI

"A resort sort of town, eighty-five kilometres away from Sibiu, no Christians. We found a room to hire (for 7 years!) and by God's grace we'll evangelise the area. Hoping to start a church - pray for Calimanesti!"

PAUCA

"16 new baptised believers! We held the service in the Cultural Hall, about 500 people present. Some came to know Christ at this service."

IN OUR LOCAL AREA

"We work for the growth of small churches, and the ones with no workers in particular. In **HUNEDOARA** - the church was almost scattered. After much prayer and visits they are doing well. **DEVA** - another Assembly had a split in the church. Some left to go elsewhere, so they were left with a small number. (Pray for DEVA, we hope to encourage them)"

***

I am certain that these reports could be repeated many times over.

Organised persecution is at the doorstep of this nation again. The Romanian Orthodox Church is flexing its muscles to oppose the preaching of the gospel of Jesus Christ.

A friend drove me to a village to see the fruits of such opposition. "When we get here", he said "you can take a photo-graph, but I will only stop for a moment. This car is known in the area and we must not aggravate the situation any more at present." I wondered what I was going to see!

As we drove, he explained the background to the problem. "Over the past year" he told me, "there were six people from this village saved. They were transported to the meeting in a neighbouring village. We decided it was time to start a new work in this village, so we bought a piece of ground in a central place and erected a concrete fence around it."

"This is the village now" he continued, as he swung the car around a gravelled village square. "There!" he said, "look at that, and take a picture quickly; the substantial concrete fence has been completely smashed!"

"How did that happen?" I asked, as I snapped the scene from the moving car.

"The priest ordered it to be broken down! He told his congregation that if any attempt was made to put a building on that ground, the 'repenters' (the six new believers) would be burned out of their houses."

"What will you do?", I enquired as we drove off in a dust cloud. He said they would leave it for a while, to see how things would develop.

As I travelled in the various provinces of Romania, I heard stories, perhaps not quite so dramatic as this one - but all of them pointed to storm clouds ahead. The Romanian believers were beginning to recognise that opposition to the Church of Christ on earth has been the story since the day when enraged men pounded Stephen to death in the stoning pit, and he became the first recorded martyr to die in the cause of His Master.

Persecution of the true Church of Jesus Christ in Romania did not end with the demise of Communism. Our Lord Jesus Christ told His followers that persecution would exist until the end of time. The word He spoke has been experienced over and over again: *"In the world ye shall have tribulation: but be of good cheer; I have overcome the world"* (John 16:33).

CHAPTER XXXIII

The Land Of The Unpredictable

---

*"Romania chastises the unwary and
rewards the intrepid"*
(Eastern Europe on a Shoestring)

This was amply illustrated in March 1994 as my friend Billy, from Northern Ireland, and I were being chauffeured from Sibiu to Brasov where we were to meet Gerald, and then drive to the church in Ploiesti for their weekly Bible teaching meeting, due to commence at six o'clock.

We left Sibiu at 12.00 noon. The weather on this trip had been very mixed, and that day was no exception. We were half way to Brasov, having just left the town of Faragas, when we were caught in a frightening thunderstorm. The rain fell like solid sheets, and it became dark as night. Just to make life more interesting, the windscreen wipers and the lights stopped working! We were forced to stop.

Half an hour later, the severity of the storm seemed to have passed, so we edged our way on to the road and continued our journey, at an unusually slow speed for a Romanian driver! It was to be a trial of patience and skill for him. When we finally approached the suburbs of Brasov, I commented that it was after four o'clock. We were two hours behind schedule.

We had planned to call for Gerald at one of the Christian homes, have a short time of fellowship, wash and change for the meeting, and leave in time to arrive at Ploiesti for the six o'clock meeting time.

This target was now outside our best efforts. In blinding rain, we made the connection with Gerald, only to find that the driver who was to take us to Ploiesti was unavailable. Gerald had been driven to the rendezvous point by an ex-patriot German-Romanian, who was on a visit to his home city. He heard of our dilemma and, at some inconvenience to himself, volunteered on the spot to drive us to Ploiesti - a two-hour journey.

The rain continued relentlessly as we transferred the luggage. We were soaked, cold and miserable! The unexpected method of transportation was a minibus-type vehicle. We left the suburbs of Brasov at 5.00 p.m., and I knew it would be impossible for us to be at the Ploiesti Assembly in time, but I made no comment.

It suddenly dawned on me that I had not been able to wash and change! "Necessity is the mother of invention", so, with the help of baby-wipes, I managed to freshen up. I took out my shirt, tie and suit from my luggage, and changed in the back of the minibus!

Six o'clock came and went - and we were less than half-way. Because of the treacherous conditions, our driver was doubly careful. "They'll think we're not coming!" I eventually commented, unable to bottle up my frustration any longer.

Gerald was deeply engrossed in a German conversation with the driver. Both of them seemed to have all the time in the world!

My friend Billy was singing!

I was uptight!

Then, quite suddenly and unexpectedly, I relaxed. I rehearsed the Scriptures that were on my heart for the meeting, and carried on into the introduction and the main body of the message. In my mind, I preached right through to the end - an exercise that made the last hour of the journey fly!

It was a bonus that I was familiar with the city of Ploiesti and the location of the unmarked Prayer House. We arrived at 7.30 p.m., one and a half hours late! I felt sure that the meeting must be over, or at least nearly over. We had resolved that we would apologise for our lateness, give greetings, and finish. Gerald said this would be the best course; that is, if they had not already given up and gone home!

But it was not to be!

Despite the heavy rain, people were standing around the open doors and windows, under plastic sheets, umbrellas, or anything that would give some protection from the elements. We were met at the door and escorted through the packed hall to the front. I apologised to one of the elders for being late.

"It is all right!" he reassured me. "We await you. Please, you must preach."

"Both of us?", I asked.

"Yes. You start now!" And so I preached and Gerald followed. We concluded the meeting at 9.30 p.m.! As usual, no one was in a hurry home; but the dampness and darkness of the evening did help to shorten the end-of-meeting greetings.

As we motored to our lodgings, I thought, 'Where in the UK would you find anything like this?'. The people would probably have given up any hope of us arriving, closed on time, and gone home!

I had always considered it highly undesirable to be late for a meeting. However, in this land of the unpredictable, our best efforts had not been sufficient to get us there on time. Apologies were brushed aside. The congregation had come to hear the Word of God, and they would not allow the time to rob them of it.

With such sacrifices, God is well pleased.

CHAPTER XXXIV

A Little Child Shall Lead Them

One of the highlights of Summer 1993 was my visit to the Harghita Camp in Northern Romania, a predominantly Hungarian area. It was unnerving to experience the subtle differences and distinctly different culture from what I was used to with the Romanian believers.

For a start, Hungarian is a most difficult language. When we travelled through Hungary in 1984 I was fascinated by the 'jaw-breaking' names on the signposts. I can recall one place-name with over thirty letters! During the ten years of travelling I never had any inclination to even try rudimentary words in Hungarian. In any case, the few believers whom I knew were able to speak excellent English.

In March 1993 Gerald and I were invited to spend some days at the Harghita Teenage Camp, to minister the word and preach the gospel. We were assured that there would be competent translators available. As with the Romanian Camp at Busteni, the majority of the time was to be given to the study of the Word, worship, prayer, and preaching the gospel.

The programme consisted of a two-hour session each morning for teaching, and in the early evening another session for praise, testimonies, preaching and teaching. In between there were discussion times and group seminars, with some space for siesta and recreation.

After a four hour journey by minibus, on not very good roads, we duly arrived at the Camp site, deep in the heart of the country, about eighty miles north of Brasov.

My friend Billy and one or two teenagers made up the numbers. On arrival we were surprised to find a very substantial building programme under way. The dormitories and four-bunk sleeping quarters were in concrete or wooden structures. The large, wooden communal hall, was capable of seating two hundred people for dining purposes. The area could be filled with rows of backless bench seats for the meetings. We were very impressed with the complex. There were also the beginnings of a small farm, which would eventually supply basic food requirements.

Gerald and I were allocated a four-bunk room, with a table and chair. It was new, tidy, and had a very pleasant outlook over the rolling countryside. The common washroom on the ground floor was Spartan but adequate. This was to be home for the next four days, and Gerald would stay on for a further three days.

Our introduction to the campers at the first meeting was very unnerving! There were over one hundred and sixty people present, their ages ranging from late teens to mid-twenties. When we entered, they were singing. It was not a Romanian sound, but it was similarly beautiful and enchanting. The song leader had a guitar strung around his neck, and he walked up and down the hall as he played and sang. The words of the songs and even the tunes were unknown to me, but my heart was touched, and I found myself holding back the tears.

There was an air of reverence in that hall; and a joy that exuded from the sea of youthful faces. I soon realised, however, that a significant number of them were not singing. They seemed a little ill at ease. It was obviously a new experience for them. I learned later that many of the young people were from colleges and universities, and had been invited to the camp by Christian colleagues. They came mainly from the Hungarian Reformed Church, and were almost totally ignorant of the gospel. During the days that followed, as we studied the Word of God together, believers and unbelievers alike were challenged. There was a remarkable movement of the Holy Spirit.

My translator was a 'stand in', as the person who was to do it had been unavoidably delayed, and would not arrive until near the end of our short stay. This young man was a student who was not really fluent in English. He just could not get on to my Irish/English wave-length! In fact, it turned out to be my most difficult experience with translation. We stumbled and sweated our way through the opening message, with frequent stops, re-runs and questionings. At the human level, it was a disaster.

After the first two sessions I decided to spend an hour or so with him before each meeting, so that we could pray together for an understanding of each other, for unity of thought and a bonding in the Spirit. Very soon I began to love this young man. He was soft-spoken, with a gentle disposition. His wife was with him at the camp, and they were obviously devoted to each other and to their Lord.

Gerald fared better! His English seemed to be easier to understand than mine, and as he preached I knew he was receiving help from the Lord.

After every meeting we would go outside, sit down in the rocky field, and sing in the darkness, under the starry heaven I have never seen such beautiful heavens as in Romania. The whole vast canopy shines with the brilliance of   millions of stars, and I would constantly find myself thinking "what an astronomical paradise!"

The singing would give way to praying. People would break off into little groups and go further into the field. By midnight there were many groups of twos, threes or fours, spread out all over the area, all in concentrated prayer.

Gerald and I walked quietly between the groups, listening to the praying voices. Though not understanding a word, we experienced an overwhelming sense of God's presence. Some were on their knees. Some were right down with their faces on the ground, crying to God with tearful, urgent intensity.

I recall a young man, one of the group from the Reformed Church. He was praying audibly, and weeping. His two Christian friends who kneeled beside him, were also weeping. We heard later than he had come to faith in Christ, and immediately he had begun to pray for his father, mother and six brothers and sisters, all of whom, he said, were "lost".

Gerald and I went to bed around midnight. Next morning we learned that the prayer meetings had continued until after 3.00 a.m.! The young people were obviously delighted; some were weeping, others laughing, as they displayed their emotions. In those few days, more than twenty trusted the Lord; and in the days that followed, Gerald remained to reap a fuller harvest. More than thirty found the Saviour. How true the words of the prophet: *"Not by might, nor by power, but by my Spirit, saith the Lord"* (Zech. 4:6). Over many years of involvement in Christian ministry, the Harghita experience must rank among the highlights. Unforgettable, and precious!

On our second day there, a leader from the Child Evangelism Fellowship arrived at the camp. He enquired if one of the 'missionaries' would come with him for two days to a nearby village, where he and a co-worker were holding a five-day Bible Club. "We would like to have you help us teach the children", was his hopeful request. Since Gerald and I were fully committed to the camp, I suggested that Billy should go. He was more than willing, and he immediately went off to put a few things into his overnight bag.

"There's not a litre of diesel to be had in this part of the county", Andrew, the CEF worker, said. "I have just about enough to get us back to the village where we are holding the meetings. I doubt very much whether I have enough to bring your friend back tomorrow, and certainly not enough to take us back to Brasov on Friday!"

"What are you going to do?", I enquired.

With a broad grin, and confidence in his voice, he said, "I've left it with the Lord. He will work something out for sure!". The conversation took place in English, so I was quite certain that I understood what he had said. He was absolutely confident that the Lord would supply the need.

When Billy returned, I said, "Brother, we had better say Good-bye, because Andrew hasn't enough diesel to bring you back here tomorrow!". This was my rather light-hearted way of dealing with a serious situation. So they set off in the traditional manner - loose stones and dust flying from the rear wheels!

Late in the afternoon of the following day, they returned. It just happened that I was there when they drove up and got out, both of them smiling from ear to ear! "Did you get diesel?", I asked.

"Praise the Lord!" responded Andrew, "Filled up to the top!"

"Where did you get it? At the Service Station?", I probed.

"No, there's still no diesel to be had!"

Billy interjected: "Drew," he said "you missed it; you really did! I have had an incredible experience. When we arrived at the village, the children had gathered to welcome us. They were so good! They sang so sweetly, and when I spoke to them about the Lord Jesus, they drank in every word."

"Later we were entertained by a local family. It was a very simple home, and I really enjoyed the fellowship and the food. Life in the village was like a hundred years ago: no roads, no footpaths, no running water, and no electricity! I was fascinated to see the ducks and drakes hopping around unrestricted in the streets. In the evening, when the sun was setting, without any obvious organisation they formed a queue and marched in procession down the street on their way home!"

"I asked Andrew how the people identified their own birds. He assured me it was no problem! But, an old Romanian friend who was with us, interrupted our conversation and spoke to Andrew in Hungarian. Andrew then said to me, 'Each evening, as the sun disappears, the birds parade down the streets like soldiers. They know their own places. The owners have no need to gather them in, or check them!'"

"That evening, with the beautiful sunset in full view, a little company gathered to sing hymns. I sang for them 'How great Thou art', 'When the Trumpet of the Lord Shall Sound' and so on. They probably didn't understand the English words, but they seemed to recognise the tunes. I will for ever remember the old people who really love the Lord Jesus, and were so happy to share their hospitality with us."

"In the morning we were to visit another village for a meeting. I said to Andrew, 'What about the diesel, what are you going to do?' We had tried several garages. No Derv! Andrew kept encouraging me - 'Trust in the Lord. He will work something out, you'll see!'"

"That morning at the children's meeting we had a prayer time with the children. Andrew explained about the empty fuel tank, and asked them to pray that the Lord would meet the need. The children prayed that God would find diesel for the missionary! When the meeting was over, one of the little girls ran home. Remembering that she had seen drums in their garden, she asked her Daddy what was in them. 'Diesel!', he said.

" 'Well, the missionary needs some. He has none, and we have been praying this morning that God would find some for him!' "

"Her father quickly said, 'Go back and bring him here, and I will give him what he needs'. So Andrew had his tank filled! And I saw the Lord intervening, with the help of a little child! When we went back for the next meeting, Andrew gathered the children together and told them that God had heard their prayer. It was lovely to see each one in turn giving thanks to the Lord."

To many this would have seemed a coincidence; but to them it was a real answer to prayer - the prayers of children! It is not surprising that, with the Precious Seed going into such good ground, many Hungarian and Romanian boys and girls are coming to the Saviour.

CHAPTER XXXV

Golgotha Mission

In the Spring of 1992 my host said to me, "I want to take you on a short journey to show you something - a plan I have for the expansion of God's work. I would like to know what you think about it, and if it would have your support!"

So Costica, Doina and I travelled eight miles south to the village of Talmaciu. I had been there often at the little Brethren church. The German brethren had left to go to Germany, and only one or two families remained. The necessary legal arrangements were made to allow the building to be handed over to the Romanian churches who, up to that time, had travelled North to Sibiu and other locations to worship. The German Scripture texts were re-painted in Romanian, and a fledgling congregation of Romanian Christians began to meet in a new fellowship. On that March morning, this was not what we had come to see.

It was a large, corner, two-storied house, with a huge overgrown garden! The owner of the house had emigrated to Germany with his family, and the property was on the market. He had installed a friend to take care of it until a new owner could be found.

We knocked the door and were admitted. As Costica conducted me through every room, and out around the garden, he shared with me his vision of a multi-purpose mission centre which would reach out to the population, over a forty to fifty mile radius.

He envisaged a small Bible School, with kitchen, dining facilities, and residential accommodation. Men and women from outlying parts, who would be the spearhead of Christian work in new areas and among the many new converts where there were no established local churches or elders to pastor them, could come and stay for short periods of intensive Bible study.

He explained that after some gospel meetings in villages, the people who were converted were influenced by Jehovah's Witnesses. Some followed them because there was no church, no teacher, no group, able to plant a permanent testimony. He said it was important to provide a facility to give in-depth Bible teaching as quickly as possible. "This is my vision", he said. "I believe it is from the Lord, and he will help us to accomplish it!"

He planned also to have it formally recognised by the Local Authorities, so that it could become a centre of spiritual and practical help to surrounding areas. There would be a small medical dispensary, stores for food and clothing; perhaps a printing room, a library, and residential accommodation for travelling servants of the Lord.

Rather shyly he shared with me that, if it was the Lord's will, he would vacate his apartment in Sibiu and come to live there with his family. As well as sharing the general concept, he produced sketches of the building extensions and alterations, which would be necessary to make the proposal viable.

I was stunned at the magnitude of the proposal, and my mind was running for cover! Up to this point I had spoken little - just a few questions to ensure I was following his thoughts correctly. Not only was I trying to take in what I was hearing, but at the same time I was endeavouring to evaluate the wisdom and the practicalities of accomplishing such an ambitious project.

Curiosity gave way to incredulity, which very quickly turned to fear. My mind was now in overdrive, and my thoughts were legion!

I had many "what ifs" and "buts"; and yet there was something about this man and his vision that captivated me. To him this was no pie-in-the-sky, no pipe-dream. He really believed in it. As a key worker in the planning of the Sibiu church, he knew the practical difficulties and imponderables that had surrounded that project. And he had seen it completed and functioning to the glory of God! Now, at great sacrifice to him and his family, he was ready to start again. A kind of Romanian Nehemiah, I thought!

He explained, "This would not be a place for diplomas or degrees. It would be a practical work place, where students could devote themselves to intensive Bible teaching, and where they would be workmen that would be taught God's truth. This would be done in the evenings and at weekends, and on one or two weeks per year there could be a full week devoted to a special topic."

"What do you think?" he asked. He waited, and I could see he longed for my approval. Ever since that night when we first met back in 1984, and solved the problem of the bus trip, I had watched this man develop and work increasingly for the Lord and for his glory.

"Drew" he urged, "we must buy the house soon. The owner wants 30,000 DM" (at that time approximately £10,000). By Western values, it was a gift. In Romanian terms, it was a fortune! He told me that the local Orthodox priest wanted to buy the property to prevent the "Cults" from getting it, so it was urgent.

I looked him in the eyes, and said as feelingly as I could, "We'll have to talk more about this, and really pray for peace in our hearts. If it is the Lord's will for us to have this house, no one else will buy it. But I cannot promise this amount of money. At present, I don't have it; and since it is the Lord's money and I am a trusted steward, I will need to be sure that the way ahead is clear."

His face fell. I knew in his heart he understood, but that did not obscure the disappointment. To ameliorate this a little I said to him, "Have a try at negotiating with the owner about a reduction in price, and let me know the outcome when I get back to Ireland."

I told him that, with certain provisos, I was sympathetic with the concept. I could see the sense and the wisdom of his thinking. He was driven by a sense of urgency and, in this new situation, he desperately wanted to find a way to equip the believers for the Lord's service.

Back home, two months later, I received a message that the owner would not reduce the price, with the question, "Have you any further thoughts about the project? The matter is urgent." After discussion with some friends and praying for guidance, I had the strong conviction that we should proceed step by step, asking the Lord to close the door if it was not His will.

I transmitted this to a colleague who was taking supplies from Northern Ireland to Romania in July, and asked him to pass on my thoughts. I had approximately 50% of the money required. When my Romanian friend got my message, he took it as the green light to proceed. One month later he telephoned me from Germany. He had travelled there with a friend to finalise the deal. Could I forward funds, by return, to the German Bank? - and he gave me the details! He had a visa for one week; and if the purchase could not be completed they would lose the sale.

I really was surprised that the negotiations had been accomplished in such a short time. It was the exception to the normal rule that I was acustomed to, in their protracted discussions and decision making. What should I do? I didn't have the full amount of money!

Two anxious days and restless nights followed. In the end, I was content that the next day would determine the outcome. And so it was that through the intervention of a friend, the money was transmitted to the bank in Germany. It arrived after the Romanians left, but a German Christian had provided the money until such times as the finance would come from Ireland. I had no difficulty in believing that it was right to purchase the house, even if the project never got off the ground. It was a sound financial investment, and if the property was not used by the church it could be resold at a much higher price! However, I believed my Romanian colleagues were motivated by the prompting of the Lord, and I had to learn to trust that all would be well.

So the work commenced. Further help came from the UK, Germany and Switzerland. The Swiss Christians, in particular, contributed not only financially, but went and gave practical help in various aspects of the construction.

"In 1993", Costica said to me, "We could see very clearly God's confirming hand in this project to help the orphanages, hospitals and surrounding communities. Unexpectedly, friends from Canada contacted us through a brother from Bucharest who had gone to live there. One night he telephoned us and told us that a Canadian family wanted to adopt a Romanian baby. They would be coming soon to Romania for this purpose, and they wondered if I could help."

"When they arrived, we looked after them and helped them to find a two-day-old baby girl. I discovered that the lady had a

Brethren background. They were deeply moved when they saw the poverty, the lack of medical supplies, and the awful conditions in the orphanages."

"When they returned home, in consultation with us, it was decided to establish an Orphanage Society under the auspices of Golgotha Mission. Shortly after the legalities were completed, a container full of medicines and medical aids arrived."

He continued, "They have told me that they will continue to supply us with medicines, etc., so that we can help the surrounding orphanages and the poor people in the villages. The work of the mission had commenced and opened doors for the gospel", he concluded.

In early 1995, the project was completed. It was a tribute to the hard work by many willing hands. The bringing in of people to be taught the Word of God was getting off the ground. So now, in this strategic part of Romania there are training, outreach, medical and conference facilities, which we pray will become a key element in the development of the Lord's work in Central Romania, and even perhaps to the more remote areas of the country.

CHAPTER XXXIV

Uracani

O ne of the most gripping parts of the Romanian saga was the widely broadcasted plight of the orphans, and the dreadful conditions in which they lived.

The majority of the orphanages are still State run, and I am told that conditions are gradually improving. Aid is coming to them from many parts of the world, and local management is benefiting from improved standards in hygiene and medical care.

A number of Christian orphanages have been established. At this time (April 1995) I am aware of three which were begun by 'the Christians According to the Gospel' (Brethren churches). They were funded and equipped in 1994 by German Christians. Now they are managed by Romanians.

The orphanage at Uracani is not functioning yet, no children have arrived to make it come alive. That is still in the future. However, preparations are well under way, and it is hoped that, in the Autumn of 1995, this small haven will be ready to receive little ones in urgent need of tender loving care, and an upbringing in a Christian environment.

The story begins in October 1992. One afternoon my door bell rang, and I opened the door to find a friend from one of the Brethren churches in Belfast. He had not been in my home before, and at that time I didn't know him very well. I invited him to come in. He held in his hand a brown envelope and as we talked together he said "The Lord has exercised my heart over the past months to do something for the orphans in Romania. Would it be possible to bring some of them to Belfast and find foster parents who could bring them up for the Lord? I would be willing to finance such a project."

I had to confess to him that I didn't think it was a good idea, and explained that, in my judgment, it was better for the Romanian orphans to be reared in their own environment and culture. Perhaps we could think about establishing a small Christian orphanage somewhere in Romania!"

"Do you think that is possible?" he queried. "I don't know", I responded, "but I can certainly find out. I will write to my contacts in Bucharest and ask them. I will let you know just as soon as I get a reply."

He said, "I want to leave this envelope with you, to go towards the initial cost of the project. Please let me know when you have a response." We prayed together, and he left.

I duly fulfilled my promise and posted a letter off to Bucharest. After two weeks I had a reply. It said, "What you have written must be of the Lord. We are thinking the same way". The writer went on to relate that the day he had received my letter he had borrowed money for the deposit on a compound with six wooden bungalows, for an orphanage! It was in the coal mining town of Uracani in Western Romania.

"The amount of money you mentioned was exactly the amount we needed to purchase the site and the houses!", he informed me.

"We are very happy about this. If you wish the brother who is donating the money to see the location, we invite both of you to come."

So in March 1993 we both set out. My friend was to stay for five days, while I planned a three-week visit. It was a torturous journey for him but he endured the extensive travel well. Finally we arrived at this almost inaccessible location, at least as far as a motor vehicle was concerned. The last one hundred meters was on foot along a dust track! "This is a terrible approach", my friend said. "Something will have to be done with this."

When I returned the following year some improvements had been made. Driving with care, it was possible to take a vehicle to the site.

This was no ordinary compound. It had been the HQ of the Securitate for the area around Uracani! Being a large coal mining area, the landscape was dominated by blocks of apartments and mine shafts dotted along the blackened hillsides. Although the general surroundings were dirty and depressing, the location was overlooked by the western end of the snow-capped Transylvanian Alps, and this view was spectacular.

I couldn't help considering the contrast between the beauty and purity of the Creator's handiwork, and the disorganised chaos and debauchery of man's creations in the valleys below. This was one of the most unpleasant towns I had ever been in, but I was informed that it was one of the wealthiest. Compared to the normal Romanian worker, the miners here made large sums of money. But they spent it all on cheap wine.

On the slopes of the rugged foothills, among the cluster of single-storey houses, a little group of us stood and prayed that one day, not too far ahead, the hillside would reverberate with the laughter of children at play - released, at last, from the incarceration of their orphan prison homes.

"Yes, this was the headquarters of the Securitate", my friend said. We could see the security fence and the observation tower extending some twenty-five metres into the air. From its top there was a commanding view of the entire valley. "The day the Revolution reached here", he continued, "the Securitate vanished. Everything is just as they left it. No one ever came back." After some time the Railway Company, whose line formed one of the boundaries, and the local Council, took over the property, and it was put on the market.

Now the Christian Brethren of Romania were its new owners!

It was decided to concentrate initially on three houses, and prepare these for a total of fifteen to eighteen children. Over the next two years, through administrative traumas, worker difficulties, and the locating of suitable staff, the houses were completely refurbished internally and insulated. A new heating plant was built and a dining area completed. The kitchen and toilet facilities were upgraded and the inside of the houses repainted.

As required by Law, twenty-one trustees have been appointed, and an Administrator is in charge of the final preparations for the reception of six children in Autumn of 1995.

The friend, who first put the idea into my mind, has fulfilled his commitment and, God willing, the orphanage will be opened free of debt. No doubt, this is a small project in a big country, but every child is precious to the Saviour. On my last visit I remember being deeply moved by the words of the Lord Jesus,

"Even so it is not the will of your Father which is in heaven,
that one of these little ones should perish"
(Matthew 18:14).

CONCLUSION

❧

When I was in Romania in 1995, I came across this unnamed testimony; and I believe it is a fitting conclusion to this story. It breathes with the devotion and fervency that characterise the ongoing evangelical witness there.

"Our Father, thank You for giving Your only begotten Son, the Lord Jesus Christ, to die on a cross - in open shame - for my sins. Forbid it, Lord, that I should boast in anything else save the death and resurrection of Christ, who is my Lord and my God. Lord Jesus, blessing and honour and glory and power and worship be unto You for ever and ever for Your precious blood in which You have washed me from my sins. Your blood is my redemption, sanctification, victory. It is every sinner's perfect plea. I am so grateful for your Holy Spirit who lives in me. I don't want to grieve him, or resist Him; I want to follow Him into all truth. Oh, how I love Your Word: may it be my meditation all the day. Please teach me to rightly divide it, and never to handle it deceitfully.

Lord, give us Your message for the people. Not my thoughts, ideas, or opinions, for I know that man's noblest effort is only dust, building on dust. You alone know who will be reading this article and only You can supply their need. So many are mixed up with troubles, doubts, fears within and without, trapped in false religions. There are those who have their hearts broken and torn apart over their marriage, children, personal problems, or are racked with pain and disease. You see the old folks, the destitute, those that are at their wits' end. They don't care about living any more. Let this be the hour when they hear Your tender voice, *"Come unto Me ... and I will give you rest." "Him that cometh to Me I will in no wise cast out."*

Father, draw them to the Lord Jesus, the only true and living God, the glorious Deliverer and the miraculous Physician. This I ask in Jesus' Name. Amen.

When we brethren preach in the parks or on the streets, repeatedly people come up afterwards to speak to us. This question pops up first almost every time:

"What religion are you?"

Of course, the constant answer is: "I am a Christian, by the grace of God".

"Yes, I know! But what denomination are you with?"

Again, "I am a Christian!".

Usually, there is sadness, a bewildered look on their faces, as if they are disappointed, or even suspicious. Why? Because the word 'Christian' has been so misused that it has lost its original meaning, and really it means nothing any more. Every fornicator, every drunkard, every idolater, every homosexual and every pickpocket in town claims to believe in God and to be a Christian nowadays!

The word Christian means Christ-like. *"The disciples were called Christians first in Antioch"* (Acts 11:26). The disciples were called Christians because they were followers of Christ, and Christ-like. As the Apostle Paul was preaching in front of King Agrippa, and reasoning with him that Christ had to suffer and was the first to rise from the dead, so that the Gentiles too might repent and turn to God, King Agrippa said *"Almost thou persuadest me to be a Christian"* (Acts 26:28). Notice he didn't say, "Almost thou persuadest me to be a Baptist, or an Orthodox, or a Pentecostal, or a Catholic ...". Christians were a specific category of people back then. Everybody knew what being a Christian meant. It was not at all popular, it involved suffering and ridicule. Yet the Bible says, *"If any man suffer as a Christian, let him not be ashamed, but let him glorify God on this behalf"* (1 Peter 4:16).

Gradually, the Gentiles labelled the disciples by the name 'Christian'. Some Jews referred to them as *"the sect of the Nazarenes"* (Acts 24:5), and Paul, when a persecutor, spoke of them as those of *"the way"* (Acts 9:2). The ending '-ianus' of the Latin word 'Christianus' was widely used in the Roman Empire, and often identified slaves with their masters. *"Paul, a servant of Jesus Christ"*; *"James, a servant of God and of the Lord Jesus Christ"*; *"Simon Peter, a servant and an apostle of Jesus Christ"* - they all considered themselves bondservants of Jesus Christ. *"The Revelation of Jesus Christ, which God gave him to show unto his servants, the things which must shortly come to pass"* (Rev. 1:1).

The Christians were not given a creed or a doctrine to proclaim. They were to exalt a Person. They were called to be ministers and witnesses unto Jesus Christ. The Lord told Paul, *"I have appeared unto thee for this purpose, to make thee a minister and a witness both of these things which thou hast seen, and of those things in the which I will appear unto thee"* (Acts 26:16). You wonder why most so-called Christians have no light from God today? That's because they are devoted to a religion, or an organisation, or a cause, and not to the Person of the Lord Jesus Christ.

True Christians are brought by the Holy Ghost into a vivid, personal, over-mastering relationship to Jesus Christ. They are *"apprehended'"* by him! (Phil. 3:12). There is nothing in their lives, apart from that personal relationship. They are absolutely Jesus Christ's. They see nothing else, they live for nothing and nobody else! *"For I am determined not to know anything among you, save Jesus Christ and him crucified"* (1 Cor. 2:2). It must be Christ first, Christ second, Christ third, until your life is *"a living sacrifice, holy and acceptable unto Him"*, and no one else is of any

212 Joy In Shared Tears

account whatever. Then your prayers and worship will be like
sweet smelling incense in God's nostrils. All the rest is pious,
religious fraud. Lord, I want only to be a Christian!

To the first Christians their own name mattered not at all. Their
concern was with the Name of Jesus Christ. Inevitably, they
became identified by the Name of Him upon whom they called,
with their hearts full of longing and adoration: Christian - Christ's
men and women. The New Testament meaning of the word alone
is adequate for us! No man is ever born a Christian. It takes the
new birth to be able to enter God's family. I am a Christian by
choice - His choice. He chose me, He won me by His love, He
bought me by His blood, and brought me to Himself by His grace.

I do not want to leave you with the impression that I think I am
the only true Christian here in Romania! I have preached in many,
many churches in this country, and I have come across many
devoted Christians.

The one point to decide is this: Will you be 'only a Christian'
too? Will you surrender to Jesus Christ, and make no conditions
whatever as to how He leads you? The passion of Christianity is
that you deliberately sign away your own rights, and become a
captive of the Lord Jesus. Until you do that, you are just pretend-
ing. You are nowhere near being a Christian!

> All to Thee, Lord, I surrender,
> All to Thee I freely give.
> I will ever love and trust Thee,
> In Thy presence daily live.

> I surrender all; I surrender all.
> All to Thee, my blessed Saviour,
> I surrender all.

APPENDIX

✑

HUMANITARIAN AID

In this story I have made one brief reference to humanitarian aid to Romania. Before closing this personal account, I feel it is only right that I should record some observations about this very important aspect of the work. Many hundreds of thousands of pounds have been contributed through individual Christians, Trusts and Churches over the eleven years of my involvement.

The Lord who sees will reward.

In the days before the Revolution there were two ways to help. The first was by the use of the "Comturist GMB" organisation, based in West Germany. They produced a small mail order catalogue which contained a range of items from food parcels, white goods, and hardware, to bicycles and motor vehicles! You simply completed the order form, stated the name and address of the recipient, enclosed a money order (which included the cost of delivery or collection at certain central points within Romania), and posted it to the firm's address in Germany. The delivery time varied from one to two months. It was costly, but effective. In the case of food parcels and small packages, these were delivered to the person concerned. For larger items, particularly vehicles, notification was sent from the factory or warehouse to the recipient, that a vehicle was there for collection.

Between 1984 and Autumn 1989 I used this method regularly, as finance became available through gifts received from individual Christians and churches, and many food parcels were sent to responsible church elders. It was impossible, of course, to correspond with the Romanian Christians, to alert them to the fact that goods were on the way. And at this time it was very difficult for them to have any means of transport, so the Comturist outlet was a very useful means to get vehicles to the people. One "Land Rover" type vehicle, manufactured by Dacia, and three Dacia cars, were purchased and delivered through their organisation.

On subsequent visits I learned that, although I had paid the full amount (including tax) for a specified vehicle, on two occasions the recipients were asked to pay more for "extras"! They did not have the money with them, so they had to return without the vehicle and borrow what was required. This information was not volunteered to me; but when I enquired, I discovered the discrepancy and was then able to make up the balance, and the loans were repaid.

The other way to help them between 1984 and 1989 was to purchase food in bulk at the Comturist Shops in Romania. They accepted only foreign currency. In some of the larger cities there would be one in the main street, but they were usually in hotels. Hotel foyers were notorious watching places for the Securitate, so it was very difficult to persuade our Romanian friends to go in to select goods from the shop. We purchased a lot of food this way, mainly flour, sugar, cheese, salami and coffee.

After the Revolution, an unexpected way suddenly opened up. Mervyn Coulson, a Northern Ireland businessman, organised the first modest transportation to Metzingen in Germany. He was travelling on business to Germany in an empty van; so it was filled with food and clothes which he left with the Romanian/German Christian community in Metzingen where they were reloaded and taken into Romania.

Following this we obtained the free use of a demonstration Hino power unit and forty foot trailer from an interested party - a Roman Catholic firm. They donated the loan of the truck, free of all charges, for three weeks!